Holly Littlewood is an experienced barrister and a member of the public law team at Spire Barristers in Leeds. Holly practises in education law and mental capacity law, and is ranked by the Legal 500 as a Leading Junior in education, Court of Protection and community care. She regularly acts in proceedings in the First-tier Tribunal (SEND) on behalf of local authorities and responsible bodies of schools, and also acts for parents. She delivers bespoke education law training to a variety of audiences, including lawyers and local authority SEND teams. Before returning to the independent bar in 2021, she worked in-house for a large local authority in their education law team.

A Practical Guide to Claims in the First-Tier Tribunal (SEND) for Disability Discrimination in Schools in England

A Practical Guide to Claims in the First-Tier Tribunal (SEND) for Disability Discrimination in Schools in England

Holly Littlewood

Barrister, Lincoln's Inn

BA (Hons), LLB, LLM

Law Brief Publishing

Published 2025 by Law Brief Publishing, an imprint of Law Brief Publishing Ltd
30 The Parks
Minehead
Somerset
TA24 8BT

www.lawbriefpublishing.com

Paperback: 978-1-916698-75-8

For R, J and F

PREFACE

Chapter 1 of Part 6 of the Equality Act 2010 ("EqA") renders it unlawful for the responsible body of a school to discriminate against a pupil or prospective pupil on the grounds of his or her disability. A claim for disability discrimination against a school situated in England must be brought in the First-tier Tribunal (SEND) ("the FTT"). The FTT only has jurisdiction to hear disability discrimination claims against the responsible bodies of schools. Claims against the responsible bodies of schools on the grounds of other protected characteristics must be made in the County Court.

Claims to the FTT differ from County Court claims in a number of important respects:

- **Accessibility:** the FTT is designed to be accessible to parents and young people who may have limited means, and / or limited access to legal advice or representation. As such, no issue fee is payable to bring a claim to the FTT, and the general rule in the FTT is no order for costs. Further, the FTT seeks to adopt a more informal and "*user friendly*" approach to proceedings than might be found in the County Court, with the aim of ensuring that parents and young people should not need to engage legal representation.
- **Procedure:** the FTT has its own distinct procedure rules. Further, it operates on an inquisitorial basis, in light of its role as a specialist tribunal.
- **Remedies:** further to a determination of disability discrimination, the FTT has a broad power to order such remedies as it thinks fit, which could include, for example, the reinstatement of a pupil who has been permanently excluded, additional tuition, or policy changes. To this extent, the FTT's power is more wide ranging than the County Court. However,

unlike the County Court, the FTT is unable to order the payment of compensation.

The volume of disability discrimination claims brought in the FTT has increased over time, rising from 190 registered appeals in the academic year 2021 / 2022[1] to 330 registered appeals in the academic year 2022 / 2023[2] (an increase of over 70 per cent). In light of the significant challenges facing the SEND system in England, it may be anticipated that the number of claims will continue to grow.

This book has been written to provide a practical, detailed guide for parties embarking upon, or responding to, a claim in this unique jurisdiction. It addresses the statutory framework and case law (including the definition of disability and the various forms of discrimination), the procedure with respect to bringing or responding to a claim in the FTT, and the framework for challenging a decision of the FTT.

Except where otherwise stated, this book addresses the law as it applies to schools situated in England. The law is believed to be accurate as of 1 September 2024.

Holly Littlewood
January 2025

---

1 Ministry of Justice, Tribunal Statistics Quarterly: July to September 2022, published 8 December 2022

2 Ministry of Justice, Tribunal Statistics Quarterly: July to September 2023, published 14 December 2023

CONTENTS

CHAPTER ONE

INTRODUCTION: THE EQUALITY ACT 2010 IN THE SCHOOL CONTEXT

The legal framework

Primary legislation

The Equality Act 2010 ("EqA") came into force on 1 October 2010, consolidating and strengthening a patchwork of pre-existing anti-discrimination laws. It provides a single legal framework to promote equality and to protect individuals from discrimination in a variety of social contexts. It applies in England and Wales, and (save for some limited exceptions[1]), in Scotland.

The EqA is a long statute, consisting of over 200 sections along with 28 Schedules. The overarching structure of the EqA, where relevant, can be summarised as follows.

Part 2 of the EqA sets out the general legal framework, including the grounds upon which an individual may experience discrimination (the "protected characteristics"), and the types of discriminatory behaviour that an individual may experience (the "prohibited conduct").

There are nine protected characteristics, seven of which are relevant to schools: disability; gender reassignment; pregnancy and maternity; race; religion or belief; sex; and sexual orientation. There are six types of

1 Section 217(2) EqA

prohibited conduct relevant to disability: direct discrimination[2]; indirect discrimination[3]; harassment[4]; victimisation[5]; discrimination arising from disability[6]; and failure to make reasonable adjustments[7] (the latter two types of prohibited conduct being unique to disability).

Parts 3 to 7 deal with specific circumstances in which such prohibited conduct is unlawful, including services and public functions; premises; work; education; and associations.

Part 8 deals with circumstances where prohibited conduct occurs in less straightforward contexts, such as where the relationship giving rise to liability has ended[8], where the prohibited conduct has been committed by an agent or employee[9], or where a third party has been instructed, caused or induced to commit prohibited conduct[10].

Part 9 sets out the various enforcement mechanisms available to claimants, which include the civil courts and the employment tribunal, depending on the context of the alleged discrimination. In the education context, jurisdiction is primarily conferred on the County Court[11], save in respect of claims brought by or on behalf of a disabled pupil or

---

2 Section 13 EqA

3 Section 19 EqA

4 Section 26 EqA

5 Section 27 EqA

6 Section 15 EqA

7 Section 21 EqA

8 Section 108 EqA 2010

9 Sections 109 – 110 EqA

10 Section 111 EqA

11 Section 114(1)(c) EqA

prospective pupil against the responsible body of a school[12] (which claims are brought instead in the First-tier Tribunal ("FTT") where the school is located in England).

Part 10 deals with the enforceability of contractual terms which are discriminatory, or which purport to exclude or limit liability under the EqA.

Part 11 deals with the advancement of equality, by setting out the public sector equality duty ("PSED"), and the circumstances in which positive action is permitted, in the recruitment and promotion context[13] and more generally[14].

Part 12 sets out specific rules with respect to disabled persons and transport.

Part 14 deals with general exceptions to the EqA.

Finally, a number of technical provisions, including general interpretation[15] and an index of defined expressions[16], can be found in **Part 16.**

Secondary legislation and guidance

The EqA is supplemented by secondary legislation. Most relevant for the purposes of this book is the *Equality Act 2010 (Disability) Regulations*

---

12 Section 116 EqA; Schedule 17 EqA

13 Section 159 EqA

14 Section 158 EqA

15 Section 212 EqA

16 Section 214 EqA

2010, which sets out supplementary provisions with respect to the definition of disability.

The EqA is also supplemented by guidance issued from a number of sources, including the Equality and Human Rights Commission ("EHRC") and relevant government departments, including the Equalities Office and the Department for Education ("DfE").

The Equalities Office[17] has issued statutory guidance in the form of the *Disability: Equality Act 2010 – Guidance on matters to be taken into account in determining questions relating to the definition of disability* (published in May 2011 and updated in March 2013) ("the Disability Guidance"). Whilst a helpful aid to the application of the EqA in certain cases, the Disability Guidance must be applied in line with the usual legal principles: it must not be "*construed as statute*", and must *"always give way to the statutory provisions"* where the two differ[18].

The EHRC has published a number of statutory codes of practice[19], in the fields of employment, equal pay, and services, public functions and associations. However, the EHRC has not published a statutory code of practice in the schools context[20]. Instead, it has published non-statutory guidance[21] in the form of *Technical Guidance for Schools in England (July 2014)* ("the Technical Guidance"). As the Technical Guidance is non-statutory, there is no statutory requirement for the FTT to take it into

17 Pursuant to the power in section 6(5) EqA

18 *Elliott v Dorset County Council* [2021] WL 1321820, paragraph 31

19 Pursuant to the power in section 14 Equality Act 2006

20 Whilst the EHRC had intended to publish a statutory Code of Practice for Schools, the government at the time decided not to lay any further draft codes before Parliament for approval (a prerequisite to the publication of a statutory Code of Practice pursuant to section 14(7) of the Equality Act 2006).

21 Pursuant to the power in section 13 Equality Act 2006

account. However, the Technical Guidance suggests that *"it may be used as evidence in legal proceedings"*, and in practice, it is often referred to in the context of an FTT case.

Finally, the DfE has published non-statutory guidance entitled *The Equality Act 2010 and Schools: Departmental Advice for school Leaders, School Staff, Governing Bodies and Local Authorities* (May 2014) ("the DfE Guidance").

Case law

Decisions of the FTT are not generally reported[22]. The case law directly considering disability discrimination in schools is largely generated by the Upper Tribunal ("UT"). Such appeals are relatively infrequent.

Much of the case law providing clarification and interpretation of the EqA arises in the context of employment claims under Part 5 EqA. The legal principles established in case law considering other spheres of activity can be of relevance to schools claims, subject to the need to consider the often fact-sensitive nature of such claims. Further, given that the EqA re-stated and strengthened the predecessor equalities legislation (including the Disability Discrimination Act 1995), case law decided under this predecessor legislation is likely to be of relevance.

Application in the school context: Part 6, Chapter 1 EqA

Schools have obligations under the EqA in a number of contexts, including where they provide services to the public (Part 3), and in their roles as employers (Part 5). This book is concerned with schools' duties to its pupils and prospective pupils (Part 6).

---

22 Although *Parents of C v Stanbridge Earls School* [2012] WLUK 136 is an unusual example of an FTT case which was reported.

Part 6, Chapter 1 EqA provides, in summary, that the responsible body of a school must not discriminate against[23] or victimise[24] a prospective pupil:

- (a) in the arrangements it makes for deciding who is offered admission as a pupil;
- (b) as to the terms on which it offers to admit the person as a pupil;
- (c) by not admitting the person as a pupil;

and must not harass a person who has applied for admission as a pupil[25].

Once a pupil is enrolled in a school, the responsible body of that school must not discriminate against[26] or victimise[27] a pupil:

- (a) in the way it provides education for the pupil;
- (b) in the way it affords the pupil access to a benefit, facility or service;
- (c) by not providing education for the pupil;
- (d) by not affording the pupil access to a benefit, facility or service;
- (e) by excluding the pupil from the school;
- (f) by subjecting the pupil to any other detriment;

and must not harass a pupil[28].

Further, the responsible body of a school is under a duty to make reasonable adjustments[29], in the context of its provisions, criteria and practices, and its provision of auxiliary aids and services (but not in relation to physical features of its premises).

---

23 Section 85(1) EqA

24 Section 85(4) EqA

25 Section 85(3)(b) EqA

26 Section 85(2) EqA

27 Section 85(5) EqA

28 Section 85(3)(a) EqA

29 Section 85(6) EqA

These obligations are widely drawn, and include a school's policies and procedures (such as those dealing with uniform, behaviour and discipline, and attendance), its curriculum delivery, break and lunchtimes, and homework, its trips, extra-curricular activities and after-school clubs, and its tests and assessments.

There are a number of important exceptions to the EqA in the schools context. For example:

- **Excluded protected characteristics**: the protected characteristics of age and marriage and civil partnership do not apply to pupils in schools[30]. Further, the protected characteristics of gender reassignment, religion or belief, and sexual orientation do not apply for the purpose of the prohibition on harassment in schools[31] (having been so excluded due to concerns about the risk of a "*chilling effect*" on Article 9 and 10 ECHR rights[32])[33].
- **Content of the curriculum**: the duties do not apply to "*anything done in relation to the <u>content</u> of the curriculum*"[34] (as opposed to the *<u>way</u>* in which the curriculum is taught[35]). This exemption has been described by the High Court as being *"cast in broad terms"*, with the intention of enabling a school *"to teach controversial material without being accused of contravening"* the EqA[36].

---

30 Section 84 EqA

31 Section 85(10) EqA

32 Joint Committee on Human Rights, Legislative Scrutiny: Equality Bill, Twenty-sixth Report of Session 2008 – 2009, paragraph 118

33 Such conduct may nonetheless amount to a detriment for the purposes of a claim of direct discrimination, pursuant to section 212(5) EqA

34 Section 89(2) EqA, emphasis added

35 Which is covered by section 85(2)(a) EqA, *per* the explanatory notes to the EqA, paragraph 302

36 *Birmingham City Council v Afsar and others* [2019] EWHC 3217 (QB), paragraphs 50 – 51

- **Collective worship**: the duties do not apply to *"anything done in connection with acts of worship or other religious observance organised by or on behalf of a school (whether or not forming part of the curriculum)"*[37].

Exceptions also apply to certain types of school (for example, in relation to single sex schools[38], schools with charitable status[39], or schools with a religious character[40]) and to admissions on the basis of a permitted form of selection[41].

Who owes duties in the school context?

All schools in England have obligations under the EqA, regardless of their management or funding arrangements. A "school" means an educational institution outside of the further or higher education sector, and which is an institution for providing primary and / or secondary education (whether or not it also provides further education)[42]. This definition includes:

- Local authority-maintained schools (including mainstream schools, maintained nursery schools[43], maintained special schools, and pupil referral units[44]);

---

37 Paragraph 6, Part 2, Schedule 11, EqA

38 Part 1, Schedule 11, EqA

39 Section 193 EqA

40 Part 2, Schedule 11, EqA

41 Paragraph 8, Part 3, Schedule 11 EqA

42 Section 4 Education Act 1996

43 NB an independent institution that provides only early years provision and is not a maintained nursery school does not fall within the definition of a school: section 4(1A) Education Act 1996.

44 Section 19(2B) Education Act 1996

- Academies (including Free Schools, Academy Special Schools, and alternative provision Academies, but excluding 16 to 19 Academies[45]);
- Independent schools (including non-maintained special schools).

Pursuant to section 85 EqA, duties are imposed on the "responsible body" of the school (often abbreviated to the "RB"), and the responsible body should be named as the respondent to any claim.

For schools maintained by a local authority, the responsible body is either the local authority or the governing body[46]. The identity of the appropriate responsible body will depend on which body was responsible for the allegedly discriminatory act. For example, the Technical Guidance suggests that a local authority which is the admissions authority for a school is likely to be the responsible body in respect of a claim in connection with admissions, whereas the governing body is likely to be the responsible body in respect of a claim in connection with a decision to exclude a pupil[47].

For other types of school, the responsible body is the proprietor[48], defined as the "*person or body of persons responsible for the management of the school*"[49]. The identity of a school's proprietor can generally be found on the DfE's online register, GIAS ("Get Information about Schools")[50].

---

45 Section 4(1B) – (1C) Education Act 1996

46 Section 85(9)(a) EqA

47 Technical Guidance, paragraph 1.7

48 Section 85(9)(b) EqA

49 Section 89 EqA; section 579(1) of the Education Act 1996

50 https://get-information-schools.service.gov.uk

Liability of responsible bodies for actions of employees and agents

Pursuant to section 109 EqA, a responsible body is vicariously liable for the actions of its employees acting in the course of their employment, and its agents acting with the responsible body's authority, whether or not such actions were taken with that responsible body's knowledge or approval[51].

Where a claim is brought against a responsible body on the basis of the actions of an employee, it is a defence to show that the responsible body took all reasonable steps to prevent the employee from carrying out the discriminatory act, or from doing anything of that description[52]. This defence is rarely used, and is available only where the responsible body can meet the high threshold of proving that **all** reasonable steps have been taken[53].

Employees are not personally liable for claims of disability discrimination in schools; as such, individual employees cannot be named as respondents to such claims[54].

Liability of responsible bodies for actions of other pupils

A responsible body will not generally be liable under the EqA for the actions or behaviours of one pupil towards another, except to the extent that it is discriminatory in its response to such actions or behaviours[55].

---

51 Section 109(1) – (3) EqA

52 Section 109(4) EqA

53 *Allay (UK) v Gehlen* [2021] 2 WLUK 57, paragraph 42

54 Section 110(7) EqA

55 DfE Guidance, paragraph 1.7

Transfer of liability upon academisation

Where a claim is brought against the governing body of a maintained school which subsequently converts to become an academy, the liabilities of the former governing body are transferred to the relevant local authority. The local authority should therefore be substituted as the respondent, and the responsible body of the academy may be added as second respondent with its consent, or may simply cooperate with the respondent local authority in the conduct of the case[56].

To whom are duties owed in the school context?

Responsible bodies owe duties to prospective and current pupils. "Pupil" has the meaning given in section 3 of the Education Act 1996; that is, a child or young person for whom education is being provided at a school, other than:

(a) *a person who has attained the age of 19 for whom further education is being provided, or*

(b) *a person for whom part-time education suitable to the requirements of persons of any age over compulsory school age is being provided.*

Pursuant to section 108 EqA, responsible bodies can in certain circumstances be liable for discrimination against former pupils, if the discrimination arises out of and is closely connected to the former pupil–school relationship. Examples of circumstances in which such liability may arise include the provision of a reference, and the provision of access to alumni communication or activities[57]. However, it is important to

---

56 *ML v Tonbridge Grammar School* [2012] UKUT 283 (AAC)

57 The Equality Act 2010 and Schools, Departmental Advice for School Leaders, School Staff, Governing Bodies and Local Authorities, May 2014, paragraph 1.8; see also the explanatory notes to the EqA, paragraph 354

note that disability discrimination claims by former pupils under section 108 EqA should be brought in the County Court and not in the FTT[58].

58 Section 114(1)(e) EqA

CHAPTER TWO

DISABILITY

There will often be little dispute that a pupil is disabled, particularly where that pupil is receiving special educational provision in school, and / or has an Education, Health and Care Plan ("EHCP"). However, whilst there is undoubtedly a significant overlap between pupils with special educational needs and pupils with a disability[59], it is also the case that a pupil may have special educational needs but no disability, or vice versa. As such, it is important to consider and apply the statutory definition of disability in each case.

Definition of disability

Section 6(1) EqA provides that a person ("P") has a disability if:

> *(a) P has a physical or mental impairment, and*
> *(b) the impairment has a substantial and long-term adverse effect on P's ability to carry out normal day-to-day activities.*

A pupil who has previously had a disability, but who has now recovered, continues to fall within this definition[60] (and therefore continues to be protected from discrimination on the basis of his or her *past* disability).

Supplementary provisions with respect to the definition of disability are set out in Schedule 1 EqA, in the Equality Act 2010 (Disability)

---

59 *Hertfordshire County Council v MC (SEN)* [2016] UKUT 385 (AAC), paragraphs 12 – 14

60 Section 6(4) EqA (save for limited exceptions which do not apply in this context)

Regulations 2010 ("the Disability Regulations"), and in statutory guidance issued under section 6(5) EqA[61] ("the Disability Guidance").

The Disability Guidance provides a number of examples where a pupil would be considered to meet the statutory definition of disability[62]:

- *A 10-year-old girl has a learning disability. She has a short attention span and has difficulty remembering facts from one day to the next. She can read only a few familiar words.*
- *A 14-year-old boy has been diagnosed as having attention deficit hyperactivity disorder (ADHD). He often finds it difficult to concentrate and skips from task to task forgetting instructions.*
- *A 12-year-old boy has cerebral palsy and has limited movement in his legs. This has a substantial adverse effect on his ability to move around the school and take part in physical sports activities.*

Physical or mental impairment

The term "impairment" should be given its "*ordinary and natural*" meaning[63]. The Disability Guidance provides that *"it is not necessary for the cause of the impairment to be established, nor does the impairment have to be the result of an illness"*[64]. Instead, *"whether a person is disabled for the purposes of the [EqA] is generally determined by reference to the* ***effect*** *that an impairment has on that person's ability to carry out normal day-to-day activities"*[65].

---

61 Disability: Equality Act 2010 – Guidance on matters to be taken into account in determining questions relating to the definition of disability, Government Equalities Office, March 2013

62 Paragraph E3

63 *McNicol v Balfour Beatty Maintenance Limited* [2002] EWCA Civ 1074, paragraph 17

64 Paragraph A3

65 Paragraph A4, emphasis *as per* original

As such, there is no legal requirement for a pupil to have a formal diagnosis in order to be classed as disabled (albeit that establishing the cause of an impairment may be helpful from an evidential perspective, where disability is a live issue[66]).

Examples of impairments given in the Disability Guidance include sensory impairments (such as those affecting sight or hearing), developmental conditions such as autism, dyslexia and dyspraxia, and mental health conditions with symptoms such as anxiety, low mood or panic attacks[67].

Certain conditions are excluded from being impairments, either for public policy reasons (for example to avoid providing protection for people whose condition may involve anti-social or criminal activity), or because they are not generally recognised as disabilities[68]. These conditions are:

- an addiction to alcohol, nicotine, or any other substance, unless originally medically prescribed[69];
- a tendency to set fires, to steal, or to physical or sexual abuse of other persons[70];
- exhibitionism and voyeurism[71]; and

[66] *Walker v Sita Information Networking Computing Ltd* [2013] WLUK 272, paragraph 16

[67] Paragraph A5

[68] Explanatory memorandum to the Equality Act 2010 (Disability) Regulations 2010, paragraph 7.3

[69] Regulation 3, Equality Act 2010 (Disability) Regulations 2010

[70] Regulation 4(1)(a) – (c), Equality Act 2010 (Disability) Regulations 2010

[71] Regulation 4(1)(d) – (e), Equality Act 2010 (Disability) Regulations 2010

- hay fever (albeit that this may be taken into account where it aggravates the effect of another, non-excluded condition)[72].

These conditions are excluded from being impairments whether they constitute an impairment in and of themselves, or whether they arise as a consequence of an impairment that otherwise constitutes a disability (for example, exhibitionism which arises as a manifestation of a pupil's ADHD)[73]. Conversely, an excluded condition may give rise to an accompanying impairment which is not excluded, and which may therefore meet the definition of disability (for example, an addiction to alcohol may lead to a physical impairment in the form of liver damage)[74]. As such, where the factual matrix includes both excluded and non-excluded impairments, it is important to pinpoint the factual basis for the alleged discrimination, in order to establish whether the protections of the EqA apply.

Prior to 2018, the effect of the "tendency to physical abuse" exception in regulation 4(1)(c) of the Disability Regulations was that disabled pupils whose conditions led them to display physically abusive behaviour in school were excluded from the protections of the EqA[75]. However, in a significant departure from the previous legal position, it was held in *C and C v Governing Body of a School*[76] that:

---

72 Regulation 4(2) – (3), Equality Act 2010 (Disability) Regulations 2010

73 Disability: Equality Act 2010 – Guidance on matters to be taken into account in determining questions relating to the definition of disability, Government Equalities Office, March 2013, paragraph A13

74 Disability: Equality Act 2010 – Guidance on matters to be taken into account in determining questions relating to the definition of disability, Government Equalities Office, March 2013, paragraph A14

75 See for example *C v Governors of a School* [2015] UKUT 7 (AAC)

76 [2018] UKUT 269 (AAC)

- regulation 4(1)(c) violated the right of children, with a recognised condition that is more likely to result in a "tendency to physical abuse", not to be discriminated against under Article 14 ECHR (prohibition of discrimination) read in conjunction with Article 2 Protocol 1 ECHR (right to education); and
- that regulation 4(1)(c) should therefore be disapplied in this context.

Pursuant to this decision, a pupil whose impairment gives rise to a tendency to physical abuse is now protected from discrimination. An example of the application of this approach can be found in *SS v Proprietor of an Independent School*[77]. In this case, it was accepted that regulation 4(1)(c) should be disapplied in respect of a claim brought on behalf of a 9-year-old pupil, S, who was permanently excluded as a result of violent and aggressive behaviour which was linked to her disabilities (which included autism, ADHD, anxiety and depression, and sensory processing difficulties).

Substantial adverse effect

"Substantial" is defined as more than minor or trivial[78]. An impairment may have a "substantial" effect on a pupil's ability to carry out normal day-to-day activities even if it does not entirely prevent him or her from carrying out such activities. Matters to consider include the length of time it takes and how difficult it is to complete an activity, and the extent to which the pupil may avoid the activity (for example, because of pain, fatigue, social embarrassment, or a loss of energy or motivation)[79].

---

77 [2024] UKUT 29 (AAC)

78 Section 212(1) EqA

79 Disability: Equality Act 2010 – Guidance on matters to be taken into account in determining questions relating to the definition of disability, Government Equalities Office, March 2013, Section B

There are a number of references in the Disability Guidance to considering whether an adverse effect is substantial by comparison with a wider cross-section of the population. For example, paragraph B1 provides that *"the requirement that an adverse effect on normal day-to-day activities should be a substantial one reflects the general understanding of disability as a limitation going beyond the normal differences in ability which may exist among people"*. Further, paragraph E2 provides that *"in considering the ability of a child aged six or over to carry out a normal day-to-day activity, it is necessary to take account of the level of achievement which would be normal for a person of a similar age"*.

However, the case law suggests that the correct way to approach this legal test is to consider what the pupil as an individual cannot do as a result of his or her physical or mental impairment[80], as opposed to comparing the pupil's ability to carry out normal day-to-day activities with the population at large[81]. As such, in *PP and SP v Trustees of Leicester Grammar School*[82], the FTT erred in considering whether a pupil's impairment (consisting of mild dyslexia and visual stress) had a substantial adverse effect on her ability carry out normal day-to-day activities by reference to average examination performance.

The appendix to the Disability Guidance provides a non-exhaustive list of examples which would and would not be reasonable to regard as having a substantial adverse effect on normal day-to-day activities. Examples of factors which it **would** be reasonable to regard as having a substantial adverse effect on normal day-to-day activities include:

- Persistent and significant difficulty in reading or understanding written material where this is in the person's native written

80 *Aderemi v London and South Eastern Railway (EAT)* [2013] ICR 591, paragraph 14

81 *Paterson v Commissioner of Police of the Metropolis* [2007] ICR 1522, paragraph 27

82 [2014] UKUT 520 (AAC)

language, for example because of a mental impairment, or learning disability, or a visual impairment (except where that is corrected by glasses or contact lenses);
- Difficulty entering or staying in environments that the person perceives as strange or frightening;
- Persistent distractibility or difficulty concentrating.

Examples of factors which it **would not** be reasonable to regard as having a substantial adverse effect on normal day-to-day activities include:
- Minor problems with writing or spelling;
- Some shyness and timidity;
- Inability to concentrate on a task requiring application over several hours.

Further relevant considerations include:
- **Corrective measures:** when assessing whether an impairment has a substantial adverse effect, any measures taken to treat or correct the impairment (such as medication, medical treatment, therapies, or other aids) should be disregarded[83]. However, this disregard does not apply to a sight impairment which is correctable by way of spectacles or contact lenses[84].
- **Progressive conditions:** where a pupil has an impairment which is caused by a progressive condition (for example, lupus or muscular dystrophy), and which has some effect on that pupil's ability to carry out day-to-day activities (albeit not yet a substantial adverse effect), then the impairment will be deemed to have a substantial adverse effect provided that this is likely to be the case in the future[85].

---

83 Schedule 1, Part 1, paragraph 5(1) – (2) EqA

84 Schedule 1, Part 1, paragraph 5(3) EqA

85 Schedule 1, Part 1, paragraph 8 EqA

- **Children under six years old:** the Disability Guidance notes that the effects of impairments may not be apparent in babies and young children because they are too young to have developed the ability to carry out activities that are normal for older children and adults[86]. As such, the Disability Regulations provide that where a pupil under six years old has an impairment which does not have a substantial and long-term adverse effect on that pupil's ability to carry out normal day-to-day activities, the impairment will be deemed to do so where it would normally have such an effect on a pupil aged six or over[87]. Children aged six and older are subject to the normal statutory definition.

Long-term

"Long-term" is defined as follows[88]:

> *(1) The effect of an impairment is long-term if—*
> *(a) it has lasted for at least 12 months,*
> *(b) it is likely to last for at least 12 months, or*
> *(c) it is likely to last for the rest of the life of the person affected.*

If an impairment ceases to have a substantial adverse effect on a person's ability to carry out normal day-to-day activities, but such an effect is likely to recur in the future, then the impairment is treated as continuing to have such an effect[89].

---

86 Paragraph E1

87 Equality Act 2010 (Disability) Regulations 2010, regulation 6

88 Schedule 1, Part 1, paragraph 2(1) EqA

89 Schedule 1, Part 1, paragraph 2(2) EqA

Normal day-to-day activities

The Disability Guidance suggests that, in general, day-to-day activities are *"things people do on a regular or daily basis"*[90], such as reading and writing, toileting, having a conversation, understanding simple instructions, moving around (including navigating stairs or slopes), and taking part in social activities. In the school context, normal day-to-day activities can include *"study and education-related activities"*[91], including *"assessments, tests, assignments,* [and] *examinations"*[92].

The Disability Guidance notes that normal day-to-day activities includes "*communication activities*", including the use of expressive and receptive language skills, and of non-verbal communication such as body language and facial expressions[93].

Deemed disabilities

A person with cancer, HIV infection, or multiple sclerosis will be deemed to be disabled[94], as will a person who is certified as blind, severely sight impaired, sight impaired or partially sighted[95]. Individuals with these conditions do not need to demonstrate that they meet the elements of the test in section 6(1) EqA (therefore making it easier for them to access the protection of the EqA[96]).

---

90 Paragraph D3

91 Paragraph D3

92 *PP and SP v Trustees of Leicester Grammar School* [2014] UKUT 520 (AAC), paragraph 23

93 Paragraph D17

94 Paragraph 6, Schedule 1 EqA

95 Regulation 7, Equality Act (Disability) Regulations 2010

96 Explanatory memorandum to the Equality Act 2010 (Disability) Regulations 2010, paragraph 7.5

An impairment which consists of a severe disfigurement (other than a body piercing or a tattoo which has not been removed) will be deemed as having a substantial adverse effect[97]. Individuals with such an impairment will only need to demonstrate that they meet the "long-term" element of the test in section 6(1)(b) EqA.

Perceived disability and discrimination by association

In certain circumstances, a claim may be brought against a responsible body by or on behalf of a pupil who is not in fact disabled. For example:

- A claim for direct discrimination under section 13 EqA may be brought on the basis that the responsible body (wrongly) perceived the pupil to be disabled[98], or on the basis that the responsible body treated a (non-disabled) pupil less favourably because of that pupil's association with a disabled person[99] (such as a sibling, parent, carer or friend)[100].
- A claim for "same disadvantage" or "associative" indirect discrimination[101] can be mounted by a non-disabled pupil under section 19A EqA, on the basis that the pupil, whilst not him or herself disabled, is put at substantively the same disadvantage as

97 Paragraph 3, Schedule 1 EqA; regulation 5, Equality Act (Disability) Regulations 2010

98 *Chief Constable of Norfolk v Coffey* [2019] EWCA Civ 1061, paragraph 35

99 *Coleman v Attridge Law and another* [2008] ICR 1128

100 It is however important to note that a claim for direct discrimination cannot be brought by a non-disabled pupil only on the basis that the responsible body has treated or would treat disabled pupils more favourably than the non-disabled pupil[100]. In this way, the EqA allows (and sometimes, pursuant to the duty to make reasonable adjustments, requires) the responsible bodies of schools to treat disabled pupils *more* favourably than non-disabled pupils.

101 *British Airways plc v Rollett*, [2024] EAT 131, paragraph 5

a group of disabled pupils by a discriminatory provision, criterion or practice.

- A claim for harassment under section 26 EqA may be brought where the conduct complained of is *"related to"* disability. This is broad in scope, and does not require the pupil to be disabled.
- A claim for victimisation under section 27 EqA is concerned with treatment connected to an individual's exercise of his or her rights under the EqA, as opposed to an individual's protected characteristic. As such, there is no requirement for a pupil to be disabled to bring a claim of victimisation against a responsible body.

For claims of discrimination arising from disability under section 15 EqA, and claims for reasonable adjustments under section 21 EqA, the "perceived disability" and "discrimination by association" provisions do not apply. As such, to bring a claim of this type, the pupil must satisfy the statutory test of disability[102].

[102] *Hainsworth v Ministry of Defence* [2014] EWCA Civ 763

CHAPTER THREE

ADMISSIONS AND EXCLUSIONS

It is unlawful for a responsible body to discriminate against or victimise a prospective pupil in the arrangements it makes for deciding who is offered or refused admission. The Technical Guidance suggests that "arrangements" for admission should be interpreted broadly, to include "*all of the policies, criteria and practices used in all of the stages of the admissions process and all admissions decisions*", including, for example, school marketing material, open events and visits, application forms, and entrance exams and interviews (where permitted)[103].

It is also unlawful for a responsible body to discriminate as to the terms on which it offers admission. In this context, the Technical Guidance provides an example of a disabled pupil who is offered only a part-time place due to concerns about the school's ability to meet the pupil's needs on a full-time basis, which would be likely to constitute discrimination arising from disability, unless justified as a proportionate means of achieving a legitimate aim[104].

There are a number of exceptions in the admissions context which are relevant to disability. Further, some decisions in respect of admissions are more appropriately challenged via alternative legal routes, as opposed to by way of a claim to the FTT. These caveats are explored in further detail below.

---

103 Technical Guidance, paragraph 2.15 – 2.16

104 Technical Guidance, paragraph 2.25

Challenging an admissions decision

Appeal to admission appeal panel

Maintained mainstream schools and the majority of Academies must comply with the detailed and prescriptive admissions regime set out Part 3 of the School Standards and Framework Act 1988 ("SSFA") and associated statutory instruments[105] and codes[106]. The Technical Guidance makes clear that nothing in the EqA requires a school to act in a way that is inconsistent with this regime[107].

A detailed discussion of the legal framework for admissions is outside of the scope of this book. However, for these purposes, it is relevant to note that Part 3 SSFA requires admissions authorities to make arrangements to enable parents to appeal a decision refusing a child admission to a maintained mainstream school. Such appeals are heard by an independent Admissions Appeal Panel. Further, whilst Academies, as independent state-funded schools, are not directly subject to Part 3 SSFA, they will generally be required by their funding agreement with the Secretary of State to comply with this legal framework[108]..

Where appeal arrangements are available in respect of an admissions decision, either under Part 3 SSFA, or under equivalent arrangements

---

105 School Admissions (Admission Arrangements and Co-ordination of Admission Arrangements) (England) Regulations 2012; School Admissions (Appeal Arrangements) (England) Regulations 2012

106 School Admissions Code, Department for Education, September 2021; School Admission Appeals Code, Department for Education, October 2022

107 Technical Guidance, paragraph 2.1

108 Unless the Secretary of State agrees to waive this requirement on the grounds of demonstrable need: see School Admissions Code, Department for Education, September 2021, paragraph 4

made pursuant to an Academy's funding agreement, then the FTT will **not** have jurisdiction to consider a challenge to the admissions decision by way of a claim of disability discrimination[109]. As such, in *AS v Buckinghamshire County Council*[110], the UT held that it did not have jurisdiction to consider a claim for failure to make reasonable adjustments in respect of a local authority administered test for selective admission to a local authority-maintained grammar school, brought on behalf of a dyslexic child who had been refused admission to that school. Instead, this claim fell within the ambit of section 94(1)(a) SSFA, and the jurisdiction of the independent Admissions Appeal Panel.

Independent schools other than Academies are not subject to the legal framework of Part 3 SSFA; as such, the only legal constraint on their admissions arrangements and decisions is the EqA.

Appeal under Part 3 of the Children and Families Act 2014

The legal framework in Part 3 SSFA does not apply to children with Education, Health and Care Plans ("EHCPs")[111]. Instead, schools admissions for this cohort are generally determined by way of the procedure in Part 3 of the Children and Families Act 2014 ("CFA")[112].

A detailed discussion of the legal framework of Part 3 CFA is outside of the scope of this book. However, it is relevant to note that this framework gives parents and young people the right to request a school of a particular type (namely a maintained school or nursery, an Academy, an FE

---

109 Schedule 17, Part 4, paragraph 13(2) EqA

110 [2010] UKUT 407 (AAC)

111 School Standards and Framework Act 1998, section 98(7), save for the exceptions set out in section 98(8) – (9)

112 Although *AB v Duke of York's Royal Military School* [2014] UKUT 403 (AAC), paragraph 32, suggests that the fact a child has an EHCP does not necessary preclude an application for admission to an Academy being made through the ordinary admissions procedure

institution, a non-maintained special school, or a section 41 approved independent special school)[113]. Where a parent or young person requests a school of one of these types, there is a rebuttable presumption that the local authority will name the school in the EHCP, unless one or more of a limited number of exceptions applies[114]. If a local authority names a school of one of these types in an EHCP, the responsible body must admit the child or young person[115].

Where a parent or young person expresses a preference for a school of a different type (such as a non-section 41 approved independent school), the local authority must take this preference into account[116]. However, there is no rebuttable presumption that such a school will be named. Further, such a school will be under no duty to admit the child or young person, even if named in an EHCP. As such, before naming such a school in an EHCP, the local authority will generally wish to satisfy itself that the school is willing and able to offer the child or young person a place.

Part 3 CFA gives parents and young people a right of appeal to the FTT against the decision of a local authority to name a particular school or type of school in an EHCP, or to name no school in an EHCP[117].

---

113 Section 38(3) Children and Families Act 2014

114 As set out in section 39(4) of the Children and Families Act 2014

115 Section 43 Children and Families Act 2014

116 In particular, the local authority must have regard to the views, wishes and feelings of the child and his or her parents, or the young person: section 19 Children and Families Act 2014; further, where the placement request is for a pupil, the local authority must have regard to the general principle that pupils are to be educated in accordance with the wishes of their parents, so far as compatible with the provision of efficient instruction and training, and the avoidance of unreasonable public expenditure: section 9 Education Act 1996

117 Section 51(2)(c)(iii) – (iv) Children and Families Act 2014

The UT case of *AB v Duke of York's Royal Military School*[118] considered the interplay between the CFA and the EqA in the context of admissions. The parents of a child ("T") issued two sets of proceedings in the FTT: an appeal under Part 3 CFA against a decision by the London Borough of Lewisham Council not to name an Academy, Duke of York's Royal Military School ("DYRMS"), in T's EHCP; and a claim under Part 6 EqA that DYRMS had discriminated against T on the grounds of his disability, by failing to give proper consideration to reasonable adjustments when assessing whether it was able to meet T's needs. The FTT held that it lacked jurisdiction to hear the EqA claim, on the basis that it was an "admissions decision" in respect of which an appeal to an independent Admissions Appeal Panel was available. T's parents appealed to the UT.

The UT agreed with the FTT that it lacked jurisdiction to hear the claim, but held that the FTT had erred in how it had reached this conclusion. DYRM had not made an "admissions decision" in respect of T; accordingly, the FTT's jurisdiction was not ousted in favour of the independent Admissions Appeal Panel. Instead, the FTT did not have jurisdiction because DYRM's actions in informing the local authority that it was unable to meet T's needs did not constitute "*arrangements __a responsible body makes__ for deciding who is offered admission as a pupil*" (emphasis added) within the meaning of section 85(1)(a) EqA.

Conceivably, the UT's decision on jurisdiction may have been different if the school under consideration was a non-section 41 approved independent school, in which circumstances, the school would have been a decision-maker (in terms of offering a school place) as well as the local authority being a decision-maker (in terms of the decision not to name the school in the EHCP).

118 [2014] UKUT 403 (AAC)

Disability-related exceptions in the admissions context

Schools with charitable status

A school which is a charity will not contravene the EqA by restricting the provision of benefits to persons who share a protected characteristic, so long as:

- The school acts in pursuance of a charitable instrument (i.e. the legal document which establishes or governs the charity[119]); and
- The provision of benefits is a proportionate means of achieving a legitimate aim, or for the purpose of preventing or compensating for a disadvantage linked to the protected characteristic[120].

This exception allows for the establishment and running of schools which cater for a particular type of disability only, to the exclusion of other types of disabled pupils (such as a school for the blind, or a school for the deaf).

Permitted form of selection

A school will not contravene the EqA on the grounds of disability "*only by applying a permitted form of selection*"[121] (emphasis added). The word "only" conveys that this exception should be construed narrowly, and should not be used to justify discrimination in admissions more generally. The forms of selection permitted under the EqA vary depending on the type of school in question.

Maintained schools can operate selective admissions arrangements as permitted under the SSFA in the following circumstances:

---

[119] Section 194(4) EqA

[120] Section 193(1)–(2) EqA; this exception does not apply to persons of a class defined by reference to colour

[121] Schedule 11, Part 3, paragraph 8 EqA

- Designated grammar schools may operate arrangements which make provision for all (or substantially all) of its pupils to be selected by reference to general ability, with a view to admitting only pupils with high ability[122].
- Pre-existing, partially selective maintained schools which are not designated grammar schools may operate arrangements for selection by ability or by aptitude where such arrangements have been in place since the beginning of the 1997 – 1998 school year[123].
- All maintained schools may operate arrangements for selection by ability for the purpose of pupil banding[124] (a system of oversubscription criteria used to ensure that the intake for a school includes a proportionate spread of children of different abilities[125]).
- All maintained schools may operate arrangements for selection by aptitude for one or more prescribed subjects[126], subject to prescribed conditions.

Independent schools can operate selective admissions arrangements which make provision for "*its pupils to be selected by reference to general or*

---

122 Schedule 11, Part 3, paragraph 8(2)(b) EqA, read with section 104 School Standards and Framework Act 1998

123 Schedule 11, Part 3, paragraph 8(2)(a) EqA, read with section 99 – 100 School Standards and Framework Act 1998

124 Schedule 11, Part 3, paragraph 8(2)(a) EqA, read with section 99 and 101 School Standards and Framework Act 1998

125 School Admissions Code, Department for Education, September 2021, paragraph 1.25

126 Schedule 11, Part 3, paragraph 8(2)(a) EqA, read with section 99 and 102 School Standards and Framework Act 1998

special ability or aptitude, with a view to admitting only pupils of high ability or aptitude"[127].

Whilst the *fact* of applying of one or more of the above permitted selective admissions arrangements to a disabled child does not constitute discrimination, this protection does not extend to *the way in which* the responsible body assesses that child's ability or aptitude. Responsible bodies remain under a duty to make reasonable adjustments to the assessment process[128] (for example, by providing an examination paper in a larger font for a visually impaired child), and to ensure that the assessment method does not indirectly discriminate against disabled children (for example, by using assessment questions that assume certain cultural or lifestyle experiences, and which may disproportionately disadvantage disabled children)[129]. However, it is important to note that the duty to make reasonable adjustments does **not** extend to altering the pass mark required[130].

This approach was endorsed by the High Court in *University of Bristol v Abrahart*[131], in the context of a higher education disability discrimination claim originating in the County Court. The High Court held that, whilst there was no duty to make reasonable adjustments to the application of a "competence standard"[132] (that is, a standard applied to measure whether a student has a particular level of competence or ability), there was in principle such a duty in respect of the methods of assessing whether a competence standard had been met[133]. It was therefore

---

127 Paragraph 8(2)(c), Schedule 11 EqA

128 Technical Guidance, paragraph 2.32

129 Technical Guidance, paragraph 2.31

130 Technical Guidance, paragraph 2.31

131 [2024] EWHC 299 (KB)

132 Schedule 13, Paragraph 4(2), EqA

133 *University of Bristol v AB* [2024] EWHC 299 (KB), paragraph 174

necessary to distinguish between the competence standard itself (in this case, explaining and defending laboratory work), and the method of assessing the competence standard (in this case, via oral communication). Whilst the former was not subject to the duty to make reasonable adjustments, the latter was.

Exclusions

It is unlawful for a responsible body to discriminate against a pupil by excluding him or her from school[134]. This includes suspensions (fixed-period exclusions) and permanent exclusions[135].

Maintained schools and Academies must follow a detailed and prescriptive procedure for excluding pupils. This procedure includes a route to appeal, first to the governing board, and then to the Independent Review Panel ("IRP"). A detailed discussion of the legal framework for exclusions from maintained schools and Academies is outside the scope of this book. However, for these purposes, it is relevant to note that nothing in the EqA requires a school to act in a way that is inconsistent with the statutory exclusions procedure. Further, compliance with the statutory exclusions procedure does not necessarily ensure compliance with the EqA[136].

Where a decision to exclude a pupil from a maintained school or Academy is tainted by disability discrimination, this decision may be challenged by way an appeal to the IRP, a claim to the FTT, or both. There are a number of differences between these two routes of appeal: one difference being the speed with which the challenge will be dealt with (IRP hearings are likely to be convened much more quickly than hearings on a claim for disability discrimination), and another difference being the

[134] Section 85 EqA

[135] Technical Guidance, paragraph 4.6

[136] Technical Guidance, 4.1

available remedies (unlike the FTT, an IRP does not have the power to order the reinstatement of the pupil). Where a parent or young person pursues both routes of appeal, the FTT claim will generally be stayed until the outcome of the IRP is known[137].

Independent schools are not subject to the statutory exclusions procedure. As such, where a decision to exclude a pupil from an independent school is tainted by disability discrimination, the only route of challenge[138] is by way of a claim to the FTT.

The FTT applies an expedited timetable to claims where a pupil has been permanently excluded and seeks an order for reinstatement. For such claims, the time allowed for the response is reduced from 30 working days to 15 working days[139], and the remainder of the directions are truncated, to allow the final hearing to take place more quickly[140].

---

137 Form SEND4: How to claim against disability discrimination in schools – a guide for parents

138 Save for any potential cause of action arising out of contract

139 Rule 21 FTT Rules

140 Form SEND4: How to claim against disability discrimination in schools – a guide for parents

CHAPTER FOUR

DIRECT DISCRIMINATION (SECTION 13 EQA)

Direct discrimination is the most conspicuous form of discrimination, in that it involves one person being treated worse than another person, because of a protected characteristic. Section 13 EqA sets out the statutory definition of direct discrimination as follows:

A person (A) discriminates against another (B) if, because of a protected characteristic, A treats B less favourably than A treats or would treat others.

As such, a claim for direct discrimination on the grounds of disability, by or on behalf of a pupil, against a responsible body, must have the following elements:

- The responsible body must have treated the pupil <u>differently</u> compared to another pupil (the "comparator" pupil).
- The responsible body's treatment of the pupil must be <u>less favourable</u> than the responsible body's treatment of the "comparator" pupil.
- The responsible body must have treated the pupil less favourably <u>because of</u> a disability.

The less favourable treatment must be because of a disability, but the pupil need not be disabled themselves[141]. For example, the less favourable treatment could be because the pupil was (wrongly) perceived to be disabled, or because of the pupil's association with a disabled person.

---

[141] *British Airways plc v Rollett and others* [2024] EAT 131, paragraph 8

In the schools context, there is no defence of "objective justification" to a claim of direct discrimination.

Claims for direct discrimination are less common in the schools context than claims for discrimination arising out of disability under section 15 EqA. This is because discrimination in school is more likely to arise out of an adverse effect which a disability has on a pupil's abilities, presentation or behaviour, as opposed to being "because of" a pupil's disability *per se*. Direct discrimination may however occur where, for example, a responsible body acts on stereotypical assumptions about a pupil's disability. An example of this situation is provided in the Technical Guidance[142] as follows:

A teacher decides to deny a pupil with a facial disfigurement a place on the school debating team, because he believes that other pupils taking part in the debates will make fun of the pupil and cause him distress. Although the teacher may think that he has good intentions, denying the pupil a chance to be on the team is likely to be direct disability discrimination.

Different treatment: the "comparator" pupil

This element of the test requires the FTT to make a comparison between the treatment which the claimant pupil has received on one hand, and the treatment which a comparator pupil has received (or would receive) on the other hand.

The comparator pupil must have materially similar circumstances to the claimant pupil (save of course for the disability which forms the basis of the claim), and in particular, must have materially similar abilities[143]. However, the pupils' circumstances need not be identical in every

[142] Paragraph 5.7

[143] Section 23 EqA

respect[144]. Instead, the question of comparability is one of fact and degree[145], and will depend on the relevance of the point of difference to the alleged less favourable treatment[146].

The comparator may be an actual pupil, or may be hypothetical. It can often be difficult to evidence how a hypothetical pupil would have been treated by a responsible body. When faced with such difficulties, the FTT may be assisted by considering an "evidential" comparator[147]; that is, a comparator who is similar, but not wholly alike, to the claimant pupil (and does not therefore satisfy the test in section 23 EqA), but whose treatment has evidential value in terms of assessing how a hypothetical comparator would be treated. Further, in some cases, the FTT may avoid the process of identifying a hypothetical comparator by focusing instead on the "reason why" the pupil was treated as he or she was[148]. If the FTT is satisfied that the pupil was treated as he or she was because of a disability, then it is likely to follow that a hypothetical comparator without a disability would have been treated more favourably.

---

144 *Chief Constable of West Yorkshire Police v Vento* [2001] IRLR 124 (EAT), paragraph 12

145 *Martin v The Board of Governors of St Francis Xavier Sixth Form College* [2024] EAT 22, paragraph 63, applying *Hewage v Grampian Health Board* [2012] UKSC 37

146 *Martin v The Board of Governors of St Francis Xavier Sixth Form College* [2024] EAT 22, paragraph 65

147 *Martin v The Board of Governors of St Francis Xavier Sixth Form College* [2024] EAT 22, paragraph 58, applying *Chief Constable of West Yorkshire Police v Vento* [2001] IRLR 124 (EAT)

148 *Shamoon v Chief Constable of the Royal Ulster Constabulary* [2003] UKHL 11, paragraph 8; *Islington London Borough Council v Ladele* [2009] ICR 387, paragraph 41

Less favourable treatment

This element of the test requires the FTT to determine, as a question of fact, whether the treatment of the claimant pupil was *less* favourable than that of the comparator pupil.

"Less favourable treatment" should be broadly construed, to include any disadvantage or detriment to which the claimant pupil has been subjected. The pupil need not have experienced any quantifiable loss or consequence[149]. For example, there is no need to demonstrate that the pupil's physical or mental health, academic progress or attainment, or disciplinary record, has been adversely affected[150]. Treatment could be "less favourable" if it involves the denial of an opportunity or choice[151], for example, to participate in an extra-curricular activity or event, or to be entered for a particular examination. The refusal of a "treat" (for example, spending additional time with a therapy dog) could in principle constitute less favourable treatment[152].

Even if the responsible body thinks the treatment is in the pupil's best interests, it may still be less favourable[153]. An example of this situation is provided in the Technical Guidance[154] as follows:

A school organises a trip to the theatre to see a Shakespeare play. The school decides that a pupil with a hearing impairment would receive greater benefit

---

149 *Shamoon v Chief Constable of the Royal Ulster Constabulary* [2003] UKHL 11, paragraph 35

150 Technical Guidance, paragraph 3.30

151 Technical Guidance, paragraph 3.30

152 *SS v Proprietor of an Independent School* [2024] UKUT 29 (AAC), paragraph 51

153 Technical Guidance, paragraph 5.46

154 Paragraph 5.7

from watching a subtitled film version of the play, so it arranges for her to stay behind at school to watch the film in the audiovisual suite. The pupil, however, would prefer to attend the theatre to see the play with her peers. Although the school may consider its intentions to be good, preventing a pupil from seeing the play at the theatre is likely to be direct disability discrimination.

The test for whether treatment is less favourable is partly, but not wholly, subjective. The pupil's perception of the treatment is likely to be a relevant consideration, and if the pupil genuinely and reasonably considers the treatment to be less favourable, then it is likely to be so[155]. However, the relevance of a pupil's views will depend on their reasonableness: an unjustified sense of grievance will not amount to a disadvantage[156].

Causation

This element of the test requires the FTT to determine the cause of, or reason for, the less favourable treatment. This is likely to require consideration of the responsible body's conscious or unconscious thought processes[157].

For the purposes of direct discrimination, the reason for the less favourable treatment must be the disability *per se*, as opposed to an adverse effect which a disability has on a pupil's abilities, presentation or behaviour. This is of course the logical outcome of the requirement for a comparator pupil with materially similar circumstances and abilities to the claimant pupil.

---

155 *Jesudason v Alder Hey Children's NHS Foundation Trust* [2020] EWCA Civ 73, paragraphs 27 – 28

156 *Shamoon v Chief Constable of the Royal Ulster Constabulary* [2003] ICR 337, paragraph 35; Technical Guidance, paragraph 5.21

157 *Pnaiser v NHS England* [2016] IRLR 170, paragraph 31

This test does not require the disability to be the sole causative factor, so long as it has a material, or significant (i.e. more than trivial), influence[158]. Further, this test does not require the responsible body to have a motive or intention to discriminate[159]. Indeed, it does not matter if the responsible body acted unconsciously[160], or with the pupil's best interests at heart[161].

Burden of proof

Claims of direct discrimination (and all other forms of discrimination) are subject to a "reverse" burden of proof, pursuant to section 136 EqA. The "reverse" burden of proof is designed to strike a fair balance as between the claimant and respondent to a claim, acknowledging that discrimination is most often covert and difficult to prove[162]. The "reverse" burden creates a two-stage process.

At the **first stage**, the burden is on the claimant to prove facts from which the FTT can conclude, in the absence of an adequate explanation, that there has been a contravention of the EqA. If the claimant fails to do so, then the claim must fail. If the claimant succeeds in doing so, then the FTT must go on to consider the second stage of the test. At the **second stage**, the burden shifts to the responsible body to prove that it did not contravene the EqA. If the responsible body fails to do so, then the FTT must uphold the claim. The standard of proof is the balance of probabilities.

---

158 *Nagarajan v London Regional Transport* [2000] 1 AC 501

159 *R (on the application of E) v JFS Governing Body* [2009] UKSC 15

160 *Chief Constable of West Yorkshire Police v Khan* [2001] UKHAL 48, paragraph 29

161 Technical Guidance, paragraph 5.7

162 *Royal Mail Group Ltd v Efobi* [2021] UKSC 33, paragraph 15

The reverse burden of proof can be particularly helpful for claimants seeking to establish a claim of direct discrimination, given that the (conscious or unconscious) thought processes of the respondent are likely to be difficult for the claimant to evidence.

Applying this two-stage process to a claim for direct discrimination, the claimant must generally first establish:

- Either, that:
    - the pupil has been treated less favourably than an actual comparator; and,
    - there is a factual basis upon which the FTT could properly infer (disregarding any other explanation) that a material factor for this treatment was a disability;
- Or, that:
    - the pupil has been treated unfavourably; and,
    - there is a factual basis upon which the FTT could properly infer (disregarding any other explanation) that a hypothetical comparator without a disability would have been treated more favourably.

The responsible body must generally then establish that disability was not a material factor for the less favourable treatment.

In terms of constructing a *prima facie* case, where a claimant identifies an actual comparator for the purposes of his or her claim, it is often helpful to also identify a hypothetical comparator, to be proposed in the alternative. This provides the claimant with a fall-back position in the event that the FTT decides that the proposed actual comparator does not meet the legal test. Further, a *prima facie* case will not usually be established simply by evidencing a difference in treatment[163]; instead, something "more" is generally required, in the form of some evidence to

[163] *Appiah v Governing Body of Bishop Douglas Roman Catholic School* [2007] EWCA Civ 10, paragraph 43

support an inference that disability was a material factor for the difference in treatment. This something more "need not be a great deal", and may in some instances be provided by the context in which the act occurred, or the responsible body's failure to give an adequate explanation for its act[164].

Although the legal test involves two stages, the FTT is not required (and should generally be discouraged) from hearing the evidence and argument on each stage separately. Instead, the FTT should look at all the relevant evidence from both parties when considering each stage[165]. Further, it may not be necessary to dwell on the role of the "reverse" burden of proof where the FTT is in a position to make positive findings on the evidence, and where inferences are not therefore required[166].

---

164 *Deman v Commission for Equality and Human Rights and others* [2010] EWCA Civ 1279, paragraph 19

165 *Royal Mail Group Ltd v Efobi* [2021] UKSC 33, paragraph 19

166 *Royal Mail Group Ltd v Efobi* [2021] UKSC 33, paragraph 38, applying *Hewage v Grampian Health Board* [2012] UKSC 37

CHAPTER FIVE

DISCRIMINATION ARISING FROM DISABILITY (SECTION 15 EQA)

This type of discrimination protects disabled pupils where the reason for the unfavourable treatment is not the disability itself, but instead is something arising from, or in consequence of, the pupil's disability[167]. Section 15 EqA sets out the statutory definition of discrimination arising from disability as follows:

> *(1) A person (A) discriminates against a disabled person (B) if—*
>
> *(a) A treats B unfavourably because of something arising in consequence of B's disability, and*
>
> *(b) A cannot show that the treatment is a proportionate means of achieving a legitimate aim.*
>
> *(2) Subsection (1) does not apply if A shows that A did not know, and could not reasonably have been expected to know, that B had the disability.*

As such, a claim for discrimination arising out of disability, by or on behalf of a pupil, against a responsible body, must have the following elements:

- The pupil must be disabled;
- The responsible body must have treated the pupil unfavourably;
- The treatment must have been for a reason (the "something");
- The reason for the treatment (the "something") must have arisen in consequence of the pupil's disability;

[167] Explanatory notes to the Equality Act 2010, paragraph 69

- The responsible body knew, or could reasonably have been expected to know, that the pupil had the disability; and,
- The responsible body cannot show that the unfavourable treatment is a proportionate means of achieving a legitimate aim (the "objective justification" defence).

It is important to note that (unlike its predecessor in section 3A of the Disability Discrimination Act 1995) there is no requirement to compare a disabled pupil's treatment with that of another, non-disabled pupil for the purposes of a claim under section 15 EqA.

The Technical Guidance[168] provides the following example of discrimination arising from disability:

A pupil with learning difficulties is not allowed to have a school meal because she has become agitated and upset whilst queuing on a number of occasions. She is asked instead to bring in a packed lunch and eat it separately, away from her friends. Her behaviour in the queue is a result of her learning difficulties. The refusal to allow the pupil to have a school meal is unfavourable treatment that is because of something that arises as a consequence of the pupil's disability.

In this example:

- The unfavourable treatment is denying the pupil a school meal with her friends.
- The reason for the treatment (the "something") is the pupil's behaviour in the queue.
- The "something" has arisen in consequence of the pupil's disability (her learning difficulties).

[168] Paragraph 5.49

- The responsible body would therefore have to show that the unfavourable treatment is a proportionate means of achieving a legitimate aim.

The EAT has held[169] that it does not matter precisely in which order the tribunal considers each element of the claim: *"It might ask first what the consequence, result or outcome of the disability is, in order to answer the question posed by "in consequence of", and thus find out what the "something" is, and then proceed to ask if it is "because of" that that A treated B unfavourably. It might equally ask why it was that A treated B unfavourably, and having identified that, ask whether that was something that arose in consequence of B's disability".* The most appropriate approach is likely to depend on the facts of the specific case.

Unfavourable treatment

This element of the test requires the FTT to determine, as a question of fact, whether the treatment of the claimant pupil was unfavourable.

As with "less favourable treatment", "unfavourable treatment" should be broadly construed, to include any disadvantage or detriment to which the claimant pupil has been subjected.

The definition of "unfavourable treatment" was considered by the Supreme Court in *Williams v The Trustees of Swansea University Pension and Assurance Scheme and another*[170]. The Supreme Court did not explicitly determine the question of whether the test for "unfavourable treatment" was purely objective (as had been held by the EAT), or whether it combined both subjective and objective elements (in line with the test for "less favourable treatment). Instead, the Supreme Court

---

169 *Basildon and Thurrock NHS Foundation Trust v Weerasinghe* [215] WL 5437262, paragraph 27

170 [2018] UKSC 65

held[171] that *"in most cases ... little is likely to be gained by seeking to draw narrow distinctions between the word "unfavourably" in section 15 and analogous concepts such as "disadvantage" or "detriment" found in other provisions, nor between an objective and a "subjective/objective" approach".*

The Supreme Court held that a "*relatively low threshold of disadvantage*" was required to meet the "unfavourable treatment" test, but that treatment which was objectively favourable to a disabled individual could not be classed as "unfavourable" simply because another disabled individual was or may have been treated even more favourably.

Because of "something"

This element of the test requires the FTT to determine the cause of, or reason for, the unfavourable treatment. As with direct discrimination, this is likely to require consideration of the responsible body's conscious or unconscious thought processes[172].

A responsible body may base its decision to treat a pupil in a particular way on multiple factors. It is not necessary for the "something" arising in consequence of the pupil's disability to be the sole or main reason for the unfavourable treatment, so long as it has a significant influence[173]. As such, in *RD and GD v The Proprietor of Horizon Primary*[174] it was an error of law for the FTT to consider only one of the reasons for a pupil being placed on a part-time timetable (the local authority's delay in naming a specialist school placement in the pupil's EHCP), and not the other reason (the pupil's behavioural difficulties).

171 Paragraph 27

172 *Pnaiser v NHS England* [2016] IRLR 170, paragraph 31

173 *Nagarajan v London Regional Transport* [2000] 1 AC 501

174 [2020] UKUT 278 (AAC)

Arising in consequence of the pupil's disability

This element of the test requires the FTT to consider whether there is a connection between whatever led to the unfavourable treatment and the pupil's disability. This element of the test is entirely objective. As such, whilst the responsible body's knowledge of the disability itself is relevant for the purposes of section 15(2) EqA, whether or not the responsible body knows that the "something" leading to the unfavourable treatment is a consequence of that disability is irrelevant[175].

"Arising in consequence of" is a relatively wide test[176]. The "something" may arise not only from the condition itself, but from the effects of the condition[177]. There may be more than one link in the chain of consequences leading back to the disability[178]. The Technical Guidance[179] provides the following guidance on the meaning of "in consequence of":

The consequences of a disability include anything that is the result, effect or outcome of a disabled pupil's disability. The consequences will be varied and will depend on the individual effect upon a disabled pupil of his or her disability. Some consequences may be obvious, such as an inability to walk unaided. Others may not be obvious, such as an inability to concentrate for

---

175 *Pnaiser v NHS England and others* [2016] IRLR 170, paragraph 31; *City of York Council v Grosset* [2018] EWCA Civ 1105, paragraph 39

176 *Basildon and Thurrock NHS Foundation Trust v Weerasinghe* [215] WL 5437262, paragraph 28

177 *RD and GD v The Proprietor of Horizon Primary (SEN)* [2020] UKUT 278 (AAC), paragraph 53, relying on *Urso v Department of Work and Pensions* [2017] IRLR 30 EAT

178 *Sheikholeslami v The University of Edinburgh* [2018] WL 04853748, paragraph 66

179 Paragraph 5.48

long periods of time, or the need for regular rest breaks or toilet breaks, or the need for instructions to be repeated or presented in visual form.

Knowledge of the disability

Pursuant to section 15(2) EqA, it is a defence for a responsible body to prove that it did not know (that is, it had no actual knowledge), and could not reasonably have been expected to know (that is, it had no constructive knowledge), that the pupil had a disability.

There are a number of important caveats to this defence. Firstly, the actual or constructive knowledge required is of the *facts* constituting the pupil's disability (that is, that the pupil has a mental or physical impairment which has a substantial and long-term adverse effect on the pupil's ability to carry out normal day-to-day activities). It is not necessary for the responsible body to appreciate that the consequence of those facts is that the pupil meets the legal definition of disability[180]. Nor is it necessary for the responsible body to have details of the pupil's precise diagnosis[181].

Secondly, there is no requirement for actual or constructive knowledge of the causal link between the pupil's disability and the "something arising" that resulted in the unfavourable treatment[182].

Thirdly, a responsible body must do all that it reasonably can be expected to do to find out whether a pupil has a disability[183]. What is reasonable will depend on the circumstances. When considering what is reasonable, a school's role in identifying and responding to SEN, as provided for in

---

180 *Gallop v Newport City Council,* [2013] EWCA Civ 1583, paragraph 36

181 *Pnaiser v NHS England and others* [2016] IRLR 170, paragraph 69

182 *City of York Council v Grosset* [2018] EWCA Civ 1105, paragraphs 39 – 40

183 Paragraph 5.54

the SEND Code of Practice: 0 to 25 Years[184], may be relevant. Where a responsible body fails to take reasonable steps to find out whether a pupil has a disability, it may be fixed with constructive knowledge. In certain circumstances, the question of whether such steps would have revealed the pupil's disability may be relevant (for example, a pupil or his or her parents chooses to conceal a pupil's disability[185]).

Objective justification

Pursuant to section 15(1)(b) EqA, it is a defence for a responsible body to prove that the treatment was a proportionate means of achieving a legitimate aim. This is often referred to as the "objective justification" test[186].

It was held by the Supreme Court in *Akerman-Livingstone v Aster Communities Ltd*[187] that the court should adopt a four-stage structured approach to the objective justification defence. The relevant questions are:

- What are the responsible body's aims or objectives in taking the relevant action?
- Is there a rational connection between the responsible body's aims or objectives and the relevant action?
- Is the relevant action no more than necessary to achieve the responsible body's aims or objectives?
- Does the relevant action strike a fair balance between the responsible body's need to achieve its aims or objective, and the disadvantage caused to the disabled pupil as a result?

---

184 See paragraph 6.14 onwards

185 *A Ltd v Z* [2019] WL 02895835, paragraph 30

186 Technical Guidance, paragraph 5.34

187 [2015] UKSC 15

In the school context, examples of legitimate aims include[188]:

- Ensuring that education, benefits, facilities and services are targeted at those who most need them;
- The fair exercise of powers;
- Ensuring the health and safety of pupils and staff, provided that risks are clearly specified;
- Maintaining academic and behaviour standards; and,
- Ensuring the wellbeing and dignity of pupils.

With respect to whether cost-cutting may constitute a legitimate aim, the Technical Guidance suggests that *"although the financial cost of using a less discriminatory approach cannot, by itself, provide a justification, cost can be taken into account as part of the school's justification if there are other good reasons for adopting the chosen practice"*[189]. This guidance is supported by the Supreme Court case of *O'Brien v Ministry of Justice*[190], which held that an aim of saving or avoiding costs cannot without more be classed as a legitimate aim, but that "costs plus" other factors may be classed as such. However, more recently, the Court of Appeal in *Heskett v Secretary of State for Justice*[191] drew a distinction between an aim which "*solely*" related to saving or avoiding costs, and an aim of "*balancing the books*" in the context of budgetary constraints. The Court of Appeal held that whilst the former was not a legitimate aim, the latter could be.

Once the first hurdle of identifying a legitimate aim is overcome, the next hurdle is to consider whether the treatment was proportionate. The UT has described this process as *"a matter of judgment for the specialist Tribunal hearing the appeal. A Tribunal makes this judgment by identifying the factors relevant to the issue and then looking at each one in the context of*

188 Technical Guidance, paragraph 5.36

189 Paragraph 5.38

190 [2013] UKSC 6, paragraph 63

191 [2020] EWCA Civ 1487, paragraph 83

the others. It must then decide whether overall, the disadvantages outweigh the benefit"[192]. When considering proportionality, the Technical Guidance suggests that *"the more serious the disadvantage … the more convincing the justification must be"*[193].

Finally, a common relevant factor for the FTT to consider is whether the responsible body has made reasonable adjustments in an attempt to obviate the need for the unfavourable treatment in question. If a responsible body fails to make reasonable adjustments for a disabled pupil, it is likely to be very difficult for it to argue that the unfavourable treatment is justified[194].

192 *RD and GD v The Proprietor of Horizon Primary (SEN)* [2020] UKUT 278 (AAC), paragraph 64

193 Paragraph 5.39

194 Technical Guidance, paragraph 5.56

CHAPTER SIX

INDIRECT DISCRIMINATION (SECTION 19 EQA)

Whereas the probation on direct discrimination aims to achieve equality of *treatment*, the prohibition on indirect discrimination aims to achieve equality of *results*. It requires a responsible body to seek to identify and remove hidden barriers in apparently indiscriminate or neutral policies or practices, in order to level the playing field for disabled pupils who would otherwise be particularly disadvantaged[195]. Section 19 EqA sets out the statutory definition of indirect discrimination as follows:

> *(1) A person (A) discriminates against another (B) if A applies to B a provision, criterion or practice which is discriminatory in relation to a relevant protected characteristic of B's.*
>
> *(2) For the purposes of subsection (1), a provision, criterion or practice is discriminatory in relation to a relevant protected characteristic of B's if—*
> *(a) A applies, or would apply, it to persons with whom B does not share the characteristic,*
> *(b) it puts, or would put, persons with whom B shares the characteristic at a particular disadvantage when compared with persons with whom B does not share it,*
> *(c) it puts, or would put, B at that disadvantage, and*
> *(d) A cannot show it to be a proportionate means of achieving a legitimate aim.*

---

[195] *Essop and others v Home Office* [2017] UKSC 27, paragraph 25

The burden of proof is on the claimant to show facts from which the FTT could decide, in the absence of any other explanation, that the first three elements of the test are made out[196]. The burden then shifts to the respondent to show that either (a) one or more of the first three elements are not made out, or (b) that the PCP can be objectively justified.

Indirect discrimination can occur where a responsible body *has applied* a provision, criterion or practice ("PCP") to a disabled pupil, or where a responsible body *would apply* a PCP to a disabled pupil in certain circumstances. This protects disabled pupils who might be deterred from doing something because of a policy which would be applied, and which would result in that disabled pupil being disadvantaged[197].

As such, a claim for indirect discrimination, by or on behalf of a pupil, against a responsible body, must have the following elements:

- The responsible body applies (or would apply) a PCP equally to everyone in a relevant group of pupils, including the disabled pupil in question;
- The PCP puts (or would put) pupils with the same disability as the disabled pupil in question at a particular disadvantage when compared with pupils who are not so disabled;
- The PCP puts (or would put) the disabled pupil in question at that disadvantage; and
- The responsible body cannot show that the PCP is a proportionate means of achieving a legitimate aim (the "objective justification" defence).

A hypothetical example of indirect discrimination is as follows:

A primary school has a policy of giving out awards and prizes in assembly to pupils who have achieved 100% attendance each term. A pupil with a

[196] *Essop and others v Home Office* [2017] UKSC 27, paragraph 33

[197] Explanatory notes to the Equality Act 2010, paragraph 79

physical disability affecting his mobility is unable to achieve 100% attendance as he needs to attend regular physiotherapy appointments during the school day. He is upset to have missed out on a prize.

In this example:

- The responsible body applies its attendance award policy equally to all pupils, including the individual pupil with the physical disability;
- The attendance award policy would put other pupils who were similarly disabled at a particular disadvantage when compared with pupils who were not so disabled;
- The attendance award policy put the individual pupil with the physical disability at a disadvantage;
- The responsible body would therefore have to show that the attendance award policy is a proportionate means of achieving a legitimate aim.

Claims for indirect discrimination are relatively rare in the context of the FTT. This is because a factual scenario which constitutes indirect discrimination is also likely, in most cases, to constitute a failure to make reasonable adjustments. In these circumstances, a claim for a failure to make reasonable adjustments is often (although not always) preferable, as it looks more narrowly at whether adjustments should be made in an individual case, rather than challenging a policy in its general application[198].

---

[198] *University of Bristol v Abrahart* [2024] EWHC 299 (KB), paragraphs 255 – 256

Provision, criterion or practice ("PCP")

The Technical Guidance[199] notes that the terms "provision", "criterion" or "practice" are not defined in the EqA, but should be interpreted widely. They may include:

- Formal or informal policies, rules, or practices;
- Arrangements (for example, deciding who to admit);
- The way in which education, or access to any benefit, service or facility is offered or provided;
- A one-off or discretionary decision; and
- A proposal or decision to do something in a particular way in the future.

The Court of Appeal in *Ishola v Transport for London*[200] held that the terms "provision", "criterion" or "practice" "*are broad and overlapping, and in light of the object of the legislation, not to be narrowly construed or unjustifiably limited in their application*"[201]. However, the Court of Appeal went on to hold that the concept of a PCP *"does not apply to every act of unfair treatment"*[202], and *"carries the connotation of a state of affairs (whether framed positively or negatively and however informal) indicating how similar cases are generally treated or how a similar case would be treated if it had occurred again"*[203]. As such, whilst a one-off decision which would be applied in the future to similarly situated pupils may constitute a PCP, a one-off decision in an individual case where there is nothing to indicate that the decision would apply in the future, is unlikely to be[204].

---

199 Paragraph 5.26

200 [2020] EWCA Civ 112

201 Paragraph 35

202 Paragraph 37

203 Paragraph 38

204 Paragraph 39

The pool for comparison

Indirect discrimination requires a comparison of the impact of a PCP on two groups:

- The group of pupils with the same disability[205] as the disabled pupil in question; and,
- A comparator group of pupils who do not have that disability[206], to whom the PCP is also applied.

When formulating the group of pupils with the same disability, the case law on formulating a group of disabled persons for the purposes of a reasonable adjustments claim may be of assistance. In *R (Rowley) v Minister for the Cabinet Office*[207], the High Court adopted the formula of *"people disabled in the same way"*, which could be a particular class (such as *"deaf persons"* or *"people with ... mobility impairments"*) or sub-class (such as *"hearing impaired people who use BSL"* or *"wheelchair users"*) [208].

For the purposes of this comparison exercise, there must be no material difference between the circumstances of the two groups[209]. It may be

---

205 Section 6(3)(b) EqA

206 The High Court in *R (Rowley) v Minister for the Cabinet Office* [2021] EWHC 2108 (Admin), paragraph 25, suggests that, for the purposes of a reasonable adjustments claim, it is preferable to compare the relevant group of disabled people with people who are not disabled, as opposed to including in the pool people with different disabilities, which risks *"introducing invidious comparisons with those who may have other disabilities, disadvantages and needs (for which different reasonable adjustments may also be necessitated)"*; see also *A Multi Academy Trust v RR* [2024] UKUT 9 (AAC), paragraph 32

207 [2021] EWHC 2108 (Admin)

208 Paragraph 24

209 Section 23(1) EqA

possible to actually identify the two groups, or they may be constructed hypothetically[210].

Disadvantage

"Disadvantage" is broadly analogous to the concepts of less favourable and unfavourable treatment considered above, and similar principles are likely to apply. It is necessary to consider:

- Whether the group of disabled pupils is (or would be) put at a disadvantage by the PCP (although it is not necessary for *every* member of the group of disabled pupils to be disadvantaged[211]); **and,**
- Whether the disabled pupil in question, as an *individual*, is (or would be) put at a disadvantage by the PCP.

There must be a causal link between the PCP and the disadvantage caused to the disabled group. Further, there must be a corresponding causal link between the PCP and the disadvantage caused to the individual disabled pupil in question[212]. As such, in the attendance award policy example above, the pupil with the physical disability would be unlikely to succeed on a claim for indirect discrimination if he had less than 100% attendance because he had been taken on a term-time holiday by his parents.

There is no requirement in law for the claimant to show *why* the PCP puts the group of disabled pupils at a disadvantage[213], although it may be easier in fact to prove group disadvantage if the reason for that

---

210 *Ishola v Transport for London* [2020] EWCA Civ 112, paragraph 36

211 *Essop and others v Home Office* [2017] UKSC 27, paragraph 27; *British Airways v Rollett and others* [2024] EAT 131, paragraph 57

212 *Essop and others v Home Office* [2017] UKSC 27, paragraph 32

213 *Essop and others v Home Office* [2017] UKSC 27, paragraph 24

disadvantage is known[214]. In some cases, the link between the PCP and the disadvantage caused to the disabled group may be obvious. In other cases, expert evidence, statistics or personal testimonies may be required[215]. As suggested in *A Multi Academy Trust v RR*[216], there may be cases where voluntary organisations dedicating to assisting those with a particular condition can help.

Objective justification

The objective justification test in section 19 EqA is substantially the same as the objective justification test in section 15 EqA (considered above), save that, under section 19 EqA, the responsible body is required to justify the general application of the PCP, whereas under section 15 EqA, the responsible body is required to justify the unfavourable treatment of an individual pupil.

"Same disadvantage" indirect discrimination

Prior to 1 January 2024, courts and tribunals were obliged, as far as possible, to interpret domestic law in accordance with principles derived from EU law ("the *Marleasing*[217] principle"). In accordance with the *Marleasing* principle, section 19 EqA had been interpreted by the Employment Appeal Tribunal in accordance with the Court of Justice of the EU case of *CHEZ Razpredelenie*[218], to permit a claimant without a relevant protected characteristic to bring a claim for indirect discrimination where they suffer alongside persons with a relevant

---

[214] *Essop and others v Home Office* [2017] UKSC 27, paragraph 33

[215] Technical Guidance, paragraph 5.24 – 5.25

[216] [2024] UKUT 9 (AAC), paragraph 29

[217] By reference to *Marleasing SA v La Comercial Internacial de Alimentación SA* (Case c-106/89) [1993] BCC 421

[218] *CHEZ Razpredelenie Bulgaria AD v Komisia za zashita ot discriminatsia* (Case C-83/14) [2015] IRLR 746

protected characteristic from a particular disadvantage arising from a discriminatory PCP[219]. This was described as "associative" or "same disadvantage" indirect discrimination.

From 1 January 2024 onwards, the Retained EU Law (Revocation and Reform) Act 2023 abolished the supremacy of EU law. In order to preserve "same disadvantage" indirect discrimination as derived from the case *CHEZ Razpredelenie*, the Equality Act 2010 (Amendment) Regulations 2023 introduced a new provision, section 19A, into the EqA[220].

Section 19A EqA provides (where relevant) that:

> (1) *A person (A) discriminates against another (B) if—*
>
> *(a) A applies to B a provision, criterion or practice,*
>
> *(b) A also applies, or would apply, the provision, criterion or practice to—*
>
> *i. persons who share a relevant protected characteristic, and*
>
> *ii. persons who do not share that relevant protected characteristic,*
>
> *(c) B does not share that relevant protected characteristic,*
>
> *(d) the provision, criterion or practice puts, or would put, persons with the relevant protected characteristic at a particular disadvantage when compared with persons who do not share the relevant protected characteristic,*
>
> *(e) the provision, criterion or practice puts, or would put, B at substantively the same disadvantage as persons who do share the relevant protected characteristic, and*

---

219 *British Airways plc v Rollett and others* [2024] EAT 131

220 Explanatory note to the Equality Act 2010 (Amendment) Regulations 2023, paragraph 1

(f) A cannot show that the provision, criterion or practice is a proportionate means of achieving a legitimate aim.

This provision allows a non-disabled pupil to bring a claim for indirect discrimination where he or she is put at substantively the same disadvantage as a group of disabled pupils by a discriminatory provision, criterion or practice. As such, to expand upon the attendance award example above:

A pupil needs to attend regular physiotherapy during the school day as part of the process of recovering from a serious injury to his hip, which has affected his mobility. He is unable to achieve 100% attendance as a result of his attendance at physiotherapy. His hip is expected to heal within a 12-month period. As such, he does not meet the statutory definition of disability.

In this example:

- The responsible body applies its attendance award policy equally to all pupils;
- The attendance award policy would put disabled pupils who needed to attend regular therapy appointments during the school day a particular disadvantage, when compared with pupils who were not so disabled;
- The attendance award policy puts the pupil with the injured hip at substantively the same disadvantage;
- It may therefore be open to the pupil with the injured hip to bring a claim under section 19A EqA to challenge the attendance award policy, notwithstanding that he is not himself disabled.

CHAPTER SEVEN

FAILURE TO MAKE REASONABLE ADJUSTMENTS (SECTION 21 EQA)

The duty to make reasonable adjustments is designed to ensure that positive steps are taken to remove or ameliorate (so far as is reasonable), the difficulties which place disabled people at a disadvantage compared to non-disabled people[221]. The duty to make reasonable adjustments has been described as a form of "*positive discrimination*"[222], the purpose of which is "*so far as reasonably practicable, to approximate the access enjoyed by disabled persons to that enjoyed by the rest of the public*"[223].

The general duty to make reasonable adjustments is set out in section 20 EqA, and comprises three requirements:

The first requirement is a requirement, where a provision, criterion or practice of A's puts a disabled person at a substantial disadvantage in relation to a relevant matter in comparison with persons who are not disabled, to take such steps as it is reasonable to have to take to avoid the disadvantage.

The second requirement is a requirement, where a physical feature puts a disabled person at a substantial disadvantage in relation to a relevant matter in comparison with persons who are not disabled, to take such steps as it is reasonable to have to take to avoid the disadvantage.

---

[221] *Secretary of State for Work and Pensions v R (MM and DM) and others* [2013] EWCA Civ 1565, paragraph 35

[222] *Archibald v Fife Council* [2004] ICR 954, paragraph 57

[223] *Roads v Central Trains Ltd* [2004] EWCA Civ 1541, paragraph 30

The third requirement is a requirement, where a disabled person would, but for the provision of an auxiliary aid, be put at a substantial disadvantage in relation to a relevant matter in comparison with persons who are not disabled, to take such steps as it is reasonable to have to take to provide the auxiliary aid.

A responsible body is under a duty to make reasonable adjustments[224] in respect of the first and third of the above requirements, and subject to the modifications set out in Schedule 13 EqA. A failure to comply with that duty in relation to a disabled pupil or prospective pupil constitutes discrimination[225]. In summary, a responsible body must comply with the following:

- A requirement:
  - (a) where a provision, criterion or practice ("PCP") applied by or on behalf of the responsible body of a school;
  - (b) puts disabled persons generally at a substantial disadvantage in relation to deciding who is offered admission as a pupil, or puts disabled pupils generally at a substantial disadvantage in relation to the provision of education or access to a benefit, facility or service;
  - (c) in comparison with persons who are not disabled;
  - (d) to take such steps as it is reasonable to have to take to avoid the disadvantage.
- A requirement:
  - (a) where, but for the provision of an auxiliary aid;
  - (b) disabled persons generally would be put at a substantial disadvantage in relation to deciding who is offered admission as a pupil, or disabled pupils generally would be put at a substantial disadvantage in relation to the provision of education or access to a benefit, facility or service;
  - (c) in comparison with persons who are not disabled;

---

224 Section 85(6) EqA

225 Section 21(2) EqA

(d) to take such steps as it is reasonable to have to take to provide the auxiliary aid or auxiliary service.

A responsible body is not under a duty to make reasonable adjustments in respect of the physical features of the school premises. It is however required to prepare an accessibility plan (which must include a plan for improving the physical environment of the school for disabled pupils[226]) and to have regard to the need to allocate adequate resources for implementing the accessibility plan[227].

The case law suggests that a *"stepped approach"*[228] should be followed when considering a claim for failure to make reasonable adjustments. The relevant stages are as follows:

- The claimant pupil must be disabled;
- The PCP or auxiliary aid must be identified;
- The group of disabled persons or pupils must be identified;
- The FTT must consider whether the PCP or absence of an auxiliary aid places disabled persons or pupils at a substantial disadvantage in comparison to those who are not disabled;
- If it does, the FTT must objectively assess whether the adjustment sought is reasonable, having identified and taken into account the nature and extent of the disadvantage[229].

---

[226] Paragraph 3, Schedule 10, EqA

[227] Paragraph 4(1), Schedule 10, EqA

[228] *R (on the application of Rowley) v Minister for the Cabinet Office* [2021] EWHC 2108 (Admin), paragraph 19

[229] *KTS v Governing Body of a School* [2024] UKUT 139 (AAC), paragraph 30

Provision, criterion or practice ("PCP") and auxiliary aids

The "PCP" formulation means the same in both section 19 and in section 20 EqA[230]. As such, the principles set out above in relation to indirect discrimination are relevant.

Examples of auxiliary aids might include adapted PE equipment, adapted keyboards and computer software[231], or Braille texts[232]. An auxiliary aid includes an auxiliary service[233]. Examples of auxiliary services might include assistance from a physiotherapist to devise suitable PE activities for a pupil who is a wheelchair user[234], or assistance from a sign language interpreter[235].

Group of disabled pupils

One important way in which Schedule 13 EqA modifies section 20 EqA is by replacing an individualised test (of whether *a* disabled person is put at a substantial disadvantage) with a group-based test (of whether disabled persons or pupils *generally* are put at a substantial disadvantage). This is different from the employment context, where the individualised test applies, and it is important to be mindful of this distinction when considering employment-related case law on this topic.

The modification of section 20 EqA to create a group-based test means that the FTT must consider the impact of the PCP or lack of an auxiliary

---

230 *Ishola v Transport for London* [2020] EWCA Civ 112, paragraph 27

231 Technical Guidance, paragraph 6.7

232 Explanatory notes to the EqA, paragraph 898

233 Section 20(11) EqA

234 Explanatory notes to the EqA, paragraph 898

235 *R (on the application of Rowley) v Minister for the Cabinet Office* [2021] EWHC 2108 (Admin)

aid on a group of disabled pupils or prospective pupils, in comparison with a non-disabled comparator group[236]. This group-based test has been described as *"a suitable trigger for what is an anticipatory duty"*[237]. As set out in the Technical Guidance, this duty requires responsible bodies to *"think in advance about what disabled pupils might require and what adjustments might need to be made for them"*[238], as opposed to solely applying adjustments for individual disabled persons on an ad hoc basis.

The formulation "disabled pupils generally" does not necessarily encompass *all* disabled pupils, but rather a particular group or class of disabled pupils. The case law suggests that this means *"people disabled in the same way"*, and could be a particular class (such as *"deaf persons"* or *"people with … mobility impairments"*) or sub-class (such as *"hearing impaired people who use BSL"* or *"wheelchair users"*)[239].

Non-disabled comparator group

The comparison is to be made with a group of non-disabled persons. The case of *A Multi Academy Trust v RR*[240] considered the question of how to formulate an appropriate comparator group of non-disabled persons in respect of a claim against a special school (in which school, there may be few, if any, actual non-disabled pupils). The UT held that the group of non-disabled persons need not be pupils at the same school, and may be hypothetical[241]. To interpret the legislation otherwise would be to

236 *A Multi Academy Trust v RR* [2024] UKUT 9 (AAC)

237 *R (on the application of Rowley) v Minister for the Cabinet Office* [2021] EWHC 2108 (Admin), paragraph 24

238 Paragraph 6.10

239 *R (Rowley) v Minister for the Cabinet Office* [2021] EWHC 2108 (Admin), paragraph 24

240 [2024] UKUT 9 (AAC)

241 Paragraphs 48–50

substantially or completely exclude pupils attending special schools from bringing reasonable adjustments claims[242].

Substantial disadvantage

"Disadvantage" is broadly analogous to the concepts of less favourable and unfavourable treatment considered above, and similar principles are likely to apply. "Substantial" means more than minor or trivial[243]. As observed in *Griffiths v Secretary of State for Work and Pensions*[244], it is particularly important in a claim for failure to make reasonable adjustments to identify the precise nature of the disadvantage caused by the PCP or absence of an auxiliary aid, in order to determine what steps might eliminate that disadvantage.

In the school context, the disadvantage which must be demonstrated is to a group of disabled pupils. It is less clear what impact must be demonstrated in respect of the individual claimant pupil. The test in section 21(2) EqA requires the failure to comply with the duty to make reasonable adjustments to be "*in relation to*" a disabled person. The question of whether the individual disabled person must suffer a detriment to bring a reasonable adjustments claim, where the nature of the reasonable adjustments duty is "anticipatory", was considered by the Court of Appeal in *R (VC) v Secretary of State for the Home Department*[245]. However, in most cases, it will not be in issue that the individual disabled pupil has experienced a disadvantage alongside the rest of the group.

242 Paragraph 51

243 Section 212(1) EqA

244 [2015] EWCA Civ 1265, paragraph 44

245 [2018] EWCA Civ 57, paragraph 172 onwards

Reasonable steps

What is "reasonable" will depend on all the circumstances. The Technical Guidance[246] identifies the following factors as relevant to the question of reasonableness:

- The extent to which special educational provision will be provided to the disabled pupil under Part 3 of the Children and Families Act 2014.
- The resources of the school and the availability of financial or other assistance.
- The financial and other costs of making the adjustment.
- The extent to which taking any particular step would be effective in overcoming the substantial disadvantage suffered by a disabled pupil.
- The practicability of the adjustment.
- The effect of the disability on the individual.
- Health and safety requirements.
- The need to maintain academic, musical, sporting and other standards.
- The interests of other pupils and prospective pupils.

The interface between the duty to make reasonable adjustments and Part 3 of the Children and Families Act 2014 is discussed further in Chapter 9 below.

There is no requirement for the pupil (or his or her parents) to have requested any particular reasonable adjustments at the relevant time, although the fact that no adjustments were requested may in some circumstances be relevant to the question of whether it was reasonable to take a particular step[247]. The claimant must, however, give some

[246] Paragraph 6.26

[247] *University of Bristol v Abrahart* [2024] EWHC 299 (KB), paragraph 163

indication as to the adjustments he or she says would have been reasonable by the time of the hearing of the claim, in order to discharge the burden of proof in section 136 EqA[248]. Further, the FTT should only consider the proposed adjustments identified by the claimant, and should not go on to consider what further, previously unidentified, adjustments ought to have been made[249].

Turning to the extent to which the steps would avoid the disadvantage, the Technical Guidance provides that it is unlikely for a responsible body to have to make an adjustment involving little benefit in reducing the disadvantage experienced by the disabled pupil. However, if this is the only possibility of avoiding the disadvantage, it may be reasonable[250]. Further, where an adjustment may have little benefit by itself, but may be of greater benefit when grouped with others, then it may be reasonable[251]. The fact that some adjustments have already been made does not mean that there is no duty to consider further or different adjustments[252].

In terms of the financial and other costs of making the adjustment, the Technical Guidance notes that if an adjustment costs little or nothing to implement, it is likely to be reasonable to do so unless some other factor (such as practicability or effectiveness) makes it unreasonable. The costs to be taken into account include those of staff and other resources. The significance of the cost of a step may depend in part on what the school might otherwise spend in the circumstances and also on what other

---

248 *University of Bristol v Abrahart* [2024] EWHC 299 (KB), paragraph 164

249 *Newcastle City Council v Spires* [2011] WL 1130026, paragraph 34

250 Technical Guidance, paragraph 6.37

251 Technical Guidance, paragraph 6.39

252 *KTS v Governing Body of a Primary School* [2024] UKUT 139 (AAC), paragraph 33

schools, in similar situations, might spend[253]. A responsible body cannot require a disabled person to contribute towards the costs of a reasonable adjustment[254].

It is not possible to justify a failure to make reasonable adjustments; as such, the key focus is likely to be whether the adjustment sought is reasonable.

The relevance of knowledge of the pupil's disability

The duty to make reasonable adjustments is anticipatory in the school context; as such, the duty exists regardless of the responsible body's actual or constructive knowledge of a particular pupil's disability, and there is no complete defence of a lack of knowledge. However, what the responsible body knew, or ought to have known, about the pupil's disability is likely to be relevant to the question of whether it was reasonable to take a particular step, and therefore, of whether the responsible body has complied with the duty in any particular case[255].

Burden of proof

Pursuant to section 136 EqA, the initial burden of proof is on the claimant to establish facts from which the FTT could decide, in the absence of any other explanation, that the duty to make reasonable adjustments has arisen (that is, that a PCP or absence of an auxiliary aid places disabled persons at a substantial disadvantage), and has been breached (that is, an indication of the adjustments which the claimant

[253] Paragraph 6.34

[254] Section 20(7) EqA

[255] *University of Bristol v Abrahart* [2024] EWHC 299 (KB), paragraph 162 – 166

says ought to have been made to avoid that disadvantage)[256]. Once the claimant has discharged this initial burden of proof, it falls to the respondent to demonstrate that the proposed adjustments would not have been reasonable.

256 *Project Management Institute v Latif* [2007] WL 1292710, paragraph 53-54

CHAPTER EIGHT

HARASSMENT (SECTION 26 EQA) AND VICTIMISATION (SECTION 27 EQA)

Harassment

Harassment is prohibited by section 26 EqA, which provides (where relevant) that:

> *(1) A person (A) harasses another (B) if—*
>
> *(a) A engages in unwanted conduct related to a relevant protected characteristic, and*
>
> *(b) the conduct has the purpose or effect of—*
>
> *(i) violating B's dignity, or*
>
> *(ii) creating an intimidating, hostile, degrading, humiliating or offensive environment for B.*
>
> *(2) …*
>
> *(3) …*
>
> *(4) In deciding whether conduct has the effect referred to in subsection (1)(b), each of the following must be taken into account—*
>
> *(a) the perception of B;*
>
> *(b) the other circumstances of the case;*
>
> *(c) whether it is reasonable for the conduct to have that effect.*

As such, a claim for harassment on the grounds of disability, by or on behalf of a pupil, against a responsible body, must have the following elements:

- The responsible body must have engaged in <u>conduct</u>;
- The conduct must be <u>unwanted</u> by the pupil;
- The unwanted conduct must be <u>related to</u> a disability;

- The unwanted conduct must have the purpose **or** effect;
- Of **either** violating the pupil's dignity, **or**, creating an intimidating, hostile, degrading, humiliating or offensive environment for the pupil ("the proscribed outcomes").

Unwanted conduct

Unwanted conduct means "unwelcome" or "uninvited" conduct[257]. This includes behaviours which are unpleasant, belittling, or bullying, and may include other actions, written or verbal comments or gestures which cause offence. There is no requirement for the pupil to demonstrate that he or she objected to the conduct[258].

The unwanted conduct must have been engaged in by or on behalf of the responsible body, as opposed to by another pupil. However, responsible bodies must ensure that they treat disability-related bullying by pupils as seriously as any other form of bullying, to ensure compliance with other provisions of the EqA[259].

"Conduct" generally implies a course of events, but can include a one-off incident if sufficiently serious[260].

Related to a disability

"Related to" has a broad meaning[261], and includes any conduct which,

---

257 Technical Guidance, paragraph 5.60

258 Technical Guidance, paragraph 5.60

259 Technical Guidance, paragraph 1.19

260 *Worcester Health and Care NHS Trust v Allen* [2024] EAT 40, paragraph 411

261 *London Borough of Haringey v O'Brien* [2016] 12 WLUK 651, paragraph 69

properly viewed, has a relationship with, or is connected to, a disability. There is no requirement for a "mental element" equivalent to that in a claim of direct discrimination for conduct to be related to a protected characteristic. Instead, conduct may be related to a protected characteristic in circumstances where the protected characteristic did not motivate the harasser, or where the harasser acted unintentionally[262].

The broad nature of the "related to" test provides protection for pupils:

- Who are themselves disabled.
- Who are wrongly perceived as disabled.
- Who are associated with a disabled person (for example, a fellow pupil or family member)[263].

The "related to" test *may* also provide protection for pupils who are known **not** to be disabled but who are nonetheless subject to harassment related to a disability. Some support for this may be found in the Court of Appeal case of *English v Thomas Sanderson Blinds Ltd*[264], which held by a majority that homophobic banter directed at a man who was known by his harassers to be heterosexual, nonetheless constituted harassment on the grounds of sexual orientation (pursuant to the *Employment Equality (Sexual Orientation) Regulations* 2003 which were at that time in force).

Purpose or effect

The unwanted conduct will constitute harassment if it has **either** the purpose, **or** the effect of producing the proscribed outcomes. The test for considering the effect of the unwanted conduct has a subjective element (the pupil's perception) and an objective element (the reasonableness of

---

[262] *Carozzi v University of Hertfordshire* [2024] EAT 169, paragraph 24

[263] Technical Guidance, paragraph 5.63

[264] [2008] EWCA Civ 1421

that perception). The objective element of the test is unlikely to be met where, for example, the pupil complaining of offensive conduct is "hypersensitive", and a "reasonable" pupil would not have been so offended[265].

Proscribed outcomes

Whether the unwanted conduct has the purpose or effect of producing the proscribed outcomes (that is of violating the pupil's dignity, or of creating an intimidating, hostile, degrading, humiliating or offensive environment for the pupil) is a matter of fact and degree. When assessing the effect of unwanted conduct, the context and circumstances of the case are likely to be highly material[266], and must be taken into account by the FTT[267].

The context and circumstances may include:

- The pupil's personal circumstances, including his or her mental health, cultural background and life experiences[268].
- The relationship between the pupil and the alleged harasser[269].
- The intention behind the unwanted conduct. Whilst it is not necessary to prove any particular intention on the part of the responsible body when relying upon the "effect" limb of the test, the intention behind the unwanted conduct may nonetheless be relevant, both as to the effect on the pupil, and the reasonableness of the pupil's perception. For example, *"the same remark may have*

[265] Technical Guidance, paragraph 5.69; see also *Richmond Pharmacology v Dhaliwal* [2009] IRLR 336

[266] *Land Registry v Grant* [2011] ICR 1390 CA, paragraph 13

[267] Section 26(4) EqA

[268] Technical Guidance, paragraph 5.68

[269] Technical Guidance, paragraph 5.68

a very different weight if it was evidently innocently intended than if it was evidently intended to hurt"[270].

- Where it is claimed that an intimidating, hostile, degrading, humiliating or offensive environment has been created, the "*general run of affairs*" including the frequency of the unwanted conduct and duration of the effect of such conduct[271].

Relationship with other types of discrimination

Section 212(1) EqA provides that "*detriment*" does not (subject to the exception set out in section 212(5) EqA) include conduct which amounts to harassment. This means that a claim for harassment on one hand, and a claim for another form of discriminatory detriment (such as direct discrimination) on the other hand, are mutually exclusive, and cannot be founded on the same facts[272]. A claimant may nonetheless wish to plead the two types of discrimination in the alternative.

Victimisation

Unlike other forms of discrimination, victimisation is not concerned with treatment related to a protected characteristic. Instead, its purpose it to protect individuals who seek to exercise their rights under the EqA. Victimisation is prohibited by section 27 EqA, which provides (where relevant) that:

(1) *A person (A) victimises another person (B) if A subjects B to a detriment because—*

(a) *B, does a protected act, or*

(b) *A believes that B has done, or may do, a protected act.*

---

270 *Richmond Pharmacology v Dhaliwal* [2009] IRLR 336, paragraph 15

271 *Weeks v Newham College of Further Education* [2012] 5 WLUK 195, paragraph 21

272 See for example *Essex County Council v Jarrett* [2015] 11 WLUK 68

(2) *Each of the following is a protected act—*

(a) *bringing proceedings under this Act;*

(b) *giving evidence or information in connection with proceedings under this Act;*

(c) *doing any other thing for the purposes of or in connection with this Act;*

(d) *making an allegation (whether or not express) that A or another person has contravened this Act.*

(3) *Giving false evidence or information, or making a false allegation, is not a protected act if the evidence or information is given, or the allegation is made, in bad faith.*

In the school context, section 27 EqA is amended by section 86 EqA to extend the definition of B to B's parent or sibling[273]. The aim of this provision is to prevent parents from being discouraged from raising an issue of discrimination due to concern that their child may suffer as a result[274].

In cases where B's parent or sibling has raised the relevant issue, it is the good or bad faith of the pupil ("B"), as opposed to his parent or sibling, which is relevant for the purposes of section 27(3) EqA[275]. As such, where the pupil's parent or sibling makes or supports a false allegation in bad faith, the pupil will still be protected by section 27 EqA where the pupil him or herself acts in good faith. Conversely, where the pupil's parent or sibling makes or supports a false allegation in good faith, the pupil will not be protected by section 27 EqA where the pupil him or herself acts in bad faith (for example, knowing the allegation to be untrue).

273 A "sibling" in this context means a brother or sister, a half-brother or half-sister, or a stepbrother or stepsister: see section 86(5) EqA.

274 Explanatory notes to the Equality Act 2010, paragraph 296

275 Section 86(3)-(4) EqA

As such, a claim for victimisation, by or on behalf of a pupil, against a responsible body, is likely to require the following elements:

- The responsible body must have subjected the pupil to a detriment.
- The responsible body must have done so because,
- The pupil, his or her parent or sibling, has done a protected act, or the responsible body believes that the pupil, his or her parent or sibling has done, or may do, a protected act.
- The pupil has acted in good faith.

The Technical Guidance[276] provides the following example of victimisation:

The stepbrother of a pupil, who is a wheelchair user, has made a complaint to his school governing body about the school not fulfilling its duty to improve the physical environment of the school for physically disabled pupils. As a result of this, the non-disabled stepsister of the pupil is not admitted into the school.

Detriment

Unlike for some other forms of discrimination, it is not necessary when considering whether a pupil has been subjected to a detriment to carry out a comparative exercise. The focus is on the pupil's experience alone (albeit that comparisons may be useful when considering the reason why the responsible body treated the pupil as it did).

As with the similar concepts of less favourable or unfavourable treatment, the term "detriment" should be widely interpreted, to include any disadvantage to which the pupil has been subject. The detriment does not have to be quantifiable, and the pupil does not have to experience

[276] Paragraph 5.79

actual loss or consequence[277]. It could for example be the loss of an opportunity or chance to do something, or anything else about which a pupil might reasonably complain[278].

Causation

The protected act (or belief that a protected act has been or may be done) must have **caused** the responsible body to carry out the detrimental treatment. This test does not require the responsible body to have a particular motive or purpose in doing so[279]. The protected act need not be the sole causative factor, so long as it has a material, or significant (i.e. more than trivial), influence[280].

Protected acts

The definition of a protect act is broad, encompassing anything done *"for the purposes of or in connection with"* the EqA, and any allegation, whether express or implied, that the responsible body or a third party has contravened the EqA. In many cases, it will be obvious whether a protected act has taken place. In cases of uncertainty, the FTT may, in appropriate circumstances, take into account the professional experience, personality and level of education of the individual doing the protected act, and whether that individual may be expected to express themselves clearly and unambiguously, or more cautiously[281].

---

277 *Shamoon v Chief Constable of the Royal Ulster Constabulary* [2003] UKHL 11, paragraph 35

278 *Chief Constable of West Yorkshire Police v Khan* [2001] UKHL 48, paragraph 53

279 *R (on the application of E) v JFS Governing Body* [2009] UKSC 15, paragraph 62

280 *Nagarajan v London Regional Transport* [2000] 1 AC 501

281 *Chalmers v Airpoint Limited* [2020] 12 WLUK 545

CHAPTER NINE

THE INTERRELATIONSHIP BETWEEN PART 6 CHAPTER 1 EQA AND OTHER STATUTORY RIGHTS AND DUTIES

Section 149 EqA: the Public Sector Equality Duty

Part 11 EqA makes provision for the advancement of equality, including by way of the Public Sector Equality Duty ("PSED")[282].

The PSED is imposed on public authorities. In the school context, this includes the governing body of a maintained school, a local authority with respect to any pupil referral units it establishes and maintains, and the proprietor of an Academy[283]. The PSED does not apply to independent schools[284]. The PSED requires such bodies to have due regard to the need to:

- Eliminate discrimination, harassment, victimisation and any other conduct that is prohibited by or under the EqA.
- Advance equality of opportunity between persons who share a relevant protected characteristic[285] and persons who do not share it.

---

282 Section 149 EqA

283 Paragraph 1, Part 1, Schedule 19 EqA.

284 *GP v The Lime Trust* [2023] UKUT 77 (AAC), paragraph 43

285 Insofar as it relates to the protected characteristic of age, the PSED does not apply to the provision of education, benefits, facilities or services to pupils in schools: see Paragraph 1, Schedule 18 EqA

- Foster good relations between persons who share a relevant protected characteristic and persons who do not share it.

Whilst the PSED can be considered an "*integral and important part of the mechanisms for ensuring the fulfilment of the aims*" of the EqA[286], it is unlikely to be of direct relevance in a disability discrimination claim in the FTT. Section 156 EqA provides that a failure to comply with the PSED does not confer a cause of action at private law. As such, it is not possible to bring a claim of disability discrimination in the FTT on this basis, and instead, such a challenge would need to be brought by way of judicial review[287].

The current edition of the Technical Guidance provides that *"a significant factor in determining whether a public authority (which includes all schools maintained by a local authority) is able to justify what may otherwise be unlawful indirect discrimination is the extent to which the public authority has complied with its public sector equality duty"*[288]. However, it was held in *GP v The Lime Trust and the Equality and Human Rights Commission*[289] that there is no requirement for the FTT to consider compliance with the PSED when determining a claim for discrimination arising from disability under section 15 EqA. In particular, a responsible body does not need to demonstrate that it has had due regard to the matters set out in section 149 EqA, in order to rely on the defence of "objective justification" under section 15(1)(b) EqA. Conversely, the fact that a responsible body has failed to comply with the PSED is not a bar

---

286 *R (Elias) v Secretary of State for Defence* [2006] EWCA Civ 1293, paragraph 274, considered in the context of the PSED in *R (on the application of TZA) v A Secondary School* [2023] EWHC 1722 (Admin), paragraph 35

287 Section 113(3)(a) EqA; see, for example, *R (on the application of TZA) v A Secondary School* [2023] EWHC 1722 (Admin)

288 Paragraph 5.41

289 [2023] UKUT 77 (AAC)

to reliance on the "objective justification" defence[290]. It remains to be seen whether the Technical Guidance will be updated accordingly in due course.

Section 88 and Schedule 10 EqA: accessibility plans

Section 88 EqA and Schedule 10 EqA require local authorities and schools to plan to make all aspects of school (including the curriculum, the physical environment, and the provision of information[291]) more accessible to disabled pupils. Pursuant to these provisions, local authorities are required to prepare an accessibility strategy for the schools for which they are the responsible body[292], and responsible bodies (of all types of school, including independent schools) are required to prepare a school-specific accessibility plan[293]. This is an important duty, particularly as the requirement to make reasonable adjustments to physical features of premises does not apply to schools[294].

Schedule 10 EqA contains its own enforcement mechanism for non-compliance by a responsible body, in the form of directions issued by the Secretary of State[295]. Further, an Ofsted inspection may include consideration of a responsible body's compliance with its duties under this Schedule[296].

---

290 Paragraph 42

291 Paragraph 1(2) and paragraph 2(2), Schedule 10 EqA

292 Paragraph 1(1), Schedule 10 EqA

293 Paragraph 2(1), Schedule 10 EqA

294 Explanatory notes to the EqA, paragraph 859

295 Paragraph 5, Schedule 10

296 Paragraph 3(7), Schedule 10, EqA

It was observed in *AB v Duke of York's Royal Military School*[297] that the FTT's jurisdiction to consider claims relating to a contravention of Part 6, Chapter 1 EqA *"appears to extend to considering whether a responsible body has failed to comply with the duty to prepare, keep under review and implement an accessibility plan in conformity with paragraph 3 of Schedule 10 to the 2010 Act, because that Schedule is introduced by section 88 which is in Chapter 1 of Part 6 of the Act"*[298]. However, it is important to note that the UT made this observation on an *obiter* basis, without the benefit of legal argument on this point. Further, the FTT's jurisdiction, as defined in paragraph 3, Part 2, Schedule 17 EqA and elucidated in the explanatory notes to the EqA[299], is to deal with *"disability discrimination claims in respect of schools pupils"* (in respect of which the relevant types of discrimination are listed in section 85 EqA).

Part 3 Children and Families Act 2014: SEND support

Part 3 of the Children and Families Act 2014 ("CFA") provides the statutory framework for identifying, assessing and supporting children and young people with special educational needs and disabilities ("SEND"), including those who have an Education, Health and Care Plan ("EHCP").

Section 42 CFA imposes a duty on the local authority to secure the special educational provision specified within an EHCP which it maintains. Section 66 CFA imposes a duty on the responsible bodies of certain types of school to use its best endeavours to secure that the special educational provision called for by a pupil's special educational needs is made (whether or not that pupil has an EHCP).

[297] [2014] UKUT 403 (AAC)

[298] Paragraph 30

[299] At paragraph 911

Part 3 CFA and Chapter 6 EqA overlap in a number of important ways, including with respect to their *"common focus on removing barriers to learning"*[300], and with respect to their shared definition of disability. However the case law suggests that, these overlaps notwithstanding, the two statutory regimes should be considered as *"entirely distinct and different"*[301].

In particular, the "*high*"[302] duty imposed on responsible bodies by section 66 CFA should not be imported into the framework of the EqA (which has its own "*modulated approach*", including considerations of reasonableness and of proportionality[303]), and should not be used to elevate the duty to make reasonable adjustments into a duty to use best endeavours. Instead, *"the duty to make reasonable adjustments is a duty that applies in the same way, and to the same standard, regardless of the nature of the school placement"*[304]. Although the framework of provision under Part 3 CFA may be relevant to considering what is reasonable by way of adjustments, it is merely one factor to consider, and carries no special weight[305].

---

300 Special Educational Needs and Disability Code of Practice: 0 to 25 Years, January 2015, paragraph 1.33

301 *RB v Calderdale Metropolitan Borough Council* [2022] UKUT 136 (AAC), paragraph 47

302 *RD and GD v The Proprietor of Horizon Primary (SEN)* [2020] UKUT 278 (AAC), paragraphs 70–71

303 *RD and GD v The Proprietor of Horizon Primary (SEN)* [2020] UKUT 278 (AAC), paragraphs 70–71

304 *KTS v Governing Body of a Community Primary School* [2024] UKUT 139 (AAC), paragraph 38

305 *SS v Proprietor of an Independent School* [2024] UKUT 29 (AAC), paragraph 77(e)

Pupils with EHCPs

The fact that a pupil has an EHCP does not exempt a responsible body from its duty to make reasonable adjustments in respect of that pupil[306]. Instead, it is necessary to identify:

- The provision required by the duty to make reasonable adjustments.
- The extent to which that provision overlaps with the provision specified in Section F of the pupil's EHCP.
- The extent to which the provision specified in Section F of the pupil's EHCP is being delivered on the ground.

In most cases, the provision required by the duty to make reasonable adjustments and the provision specified in Section F of the pupil's EHCP will be the same. Where there is complete overlap between the two types of provision, and where the provision has been secured via the EHCP, then no additional steps are required by the responsible body to discharge its duty to make reasonable adjustments.

An example of this situation is provided in the Technical Guidance as follows:

A disabled pupil has an EHC plan and attends a maintained mainstream secondary school. Through her EHC plan, she receives two hours a week of specialist teaching and uses an electronic notetaker in lessons. Because the support that she requires is provided through her EHC plan, the school does not therefore have to make reasonable adjustments by providing these auxiliary aids and services for her.[307]

---

306 *SS v Proprietor of an Independent School* [2024] UKUT 29 (AAC), paragraph 77(a)

307 Technical Guidance, paragraph 6.28

However, the provision required by the duty to make reasonable adjustments and the provision specified in the pupil's EHCP may not completely align. For example, a pupil may have special educational needs which require special educational provision to be made in accordance with an EHCP, and may also have a disability which does not call for special educational provision, but in respect of which that pupil requires reasonable adjustments. In this circumstance, the responsible body would be required to make additional provision, over and above the provision secured under the pupil's EHCP, in order to fully discharge its duty to make reasonable adjustments.

An example of this situation is provided in the Technical Guidance as follows:

An infant school disabled pupil with attention deficit hyperactivity disorder (ADHD) receives some individual teaching assistant support through the SEN framework. He is diagnosed with severe asthma and needs assistance with his nebuliser. Although this is not a special educational need, his asthma is likely to be a disability for the purpose of the Act and so a failure to provide a reasonable adjustment will place him at a substantial disadvantage. The school trains his teaching assistant and she provides him with the assistance that he needs. This would be a reasonable adjustment for the school to make[308].

Further, a responsible body may be in breach of its duty to make reasonable adjustments where the provision specified in Section F of a pupil's ECHP is not being delivered on the ground. As held in *KTS v Governing Body of a Primary School*[309], *"in most cases, what is specified in Section F will be provision that is also required by the duty to make reasonable adjustments because, by statutory definition, it should be the provision*

---

[308] Technical Guidance, paragraph 6.29

[309] *KTS v Governing Body of a Community Primary School* [2024] UKUT 139 (AAC), paragraph 38

reasonably required to remove the disadvantage that the child is under in relation to their peers. The provision in Section F and the provision required by the duty to make reasonable adjustments will, in particular, normally be the same where the provision in the EHCP consists of teaching approaches, strategies and resources that would ordinarily be provided by a school from within its own resources". As such, *"in the ordinary course of events, a school that fails to implement the teaching approaches, strategies and resources specified in the EHCP as being required for the child is likely also to be failing in its duty to make reasonable adjustments".*

However, a failure in the delivery of provision under an EHCP will not automatically constitute a failure by the responsible body to make reasonable adjustments. For example, it may not do so where *"the provision in the EHCP is out of date or unreasonable in some other respect, or [if] in fact the child is not at a substantial disadvantage in relation to that particular matter"*[310]. Further, where an EHCP makes provision for a pupil to receive support from another agency, it is unlikely to be reasonable to expect the responsible body to duplicate that support[311]. That said, where there has been a failure by a local authority to secure provision under an EHCP, the FTT must consider whether it is reasonable for the school to "bridge the gap" by making the adjustments that would otherwise be secured by the local authority. When considering what is reasonable, the length of time for which the "bridging" measures are required may be relevant[312].

A claim for failure to make reasonable adjustments under the EqA not will necessarily be the most appropriate way of enforcing a failure to

---

310 *KTS v Governing Body of a Community Primary School* [2024] UKUT 139 (AAC), paragraph 38

311 *KTS v Governing Body of a Community Primary School* [2024] UKUT 139 (AAC), paragraph 38; Technical Guidance, paragraph 6.31

312 *SS v Proprietor of an Independent School* [2024] UKUT 29 (AAC), paragraph 77(i)

make the provision specified in the EHCP, even if technically available[313]. As held in *KTS v Governing Body of a Primary School*[314], *"informal resolution and, if necessary, mediation should always be the starting point. Judicial review proceedings may be more appropriate in some cases, particularly perhaps where there may be joint responsibility for the failure as between the local authority and the school"*. Further, consideration must be given to whether each element of the statutory test for a claim for failure to make reasonable adjustments is met: such a claim cannot be presented as *"a generalised claim for enforcement of the EHCP"*.

Independent schools

Although the responsible body of an independent school is not subject to the duty to use its best endeavours to secure special educational provision pursuant to section 66 CFA, it is not excepted from the duty to make reasonable adjustments under sections 20–21 EqA[315]. This remains the case even where a child's parents have decided to place the child in an independent school other than the school named in Section I of the child's EHCP, and where the local authority is treating its duty to secure special educational provision as discharged on that basis[316].

In such a case, the FTT may conclude that the adjustments sought are not reasonable because "*the substantial disadvantage could potentially be avoided by securing local authority-funded provision through and EHCP or by the child moving to the school named in the EHCP (albeit that the Tribunal will need to take into account that the child will thereby also lose*

---

313 *KTS v Governing Body of a Community Primary School* [2024] UKUT 139 (AAC), paragraph 38

314 [2024] UKUT 139 (AAC), paragraph 38

315 *SS v Proprietor of an Independent School* [2024] UKUT 29 (AAC), paragraph 77(b) and (e)

316 *SS v Proprietor of an Independent School* [2024] UKUT 29 (AAC), paragraph 77(d)

what the parents are likely to see as the significant benefits of a private education)". Alternatively, the FTT may conclude that the adjustments sought are reasonable despite the child's parents having *"the option of taking up the local authority-funded provision available to the child through the EHCP"*[317].

Section 2 of the Education Act 1996: entitlement to a full-time education

In general terms, and subject to exceptions, a pupil of compulsory school age is entitled by section 2 of the Education Act 1996 to a suitable, full-time education. In certain, limited, circumstances, a responsible body may decide to provide a pupil of compulsory school age with a temporary part-time timetable[318]. However, where a pupil is provided with a part-time timetable because of something arising in consequence of his or her disability, then pursuant to section 15 EqA, this will constitute discrimination unless objectively justified. The interface between the entitlement to a full-time education under the Education Act 1996 and the objective justification exercise in section 15 EqA has been considered in two UT cases.

In the case of *F-T v The Governors of Hampton Dene Primary School (SEN)*[319], it was held that the fact a pupil had been denied the full-time schooling to which she was entitled under the Education Act 1996 was *"a matter of central importance"* to the question of proportionality. However, in the subsequent case of *RD and GD v The Proprietor of Horizon Primary (SEN)*[320], the UT disagreed. Instead, the UT held that the objective justification exercise requires the FTT *"to look at each factor*

317 *SS v Proprietor of an Independent School* [2024] UKUT 29 (AAC), paragraph 77(h)

318 See paragraphs 65–70 of the statutory guidance *Working Together to Improve School Attendance,* Department for Education, August 2024

319 [2016] UKUT 468 (AAC), paragraph 59

320 [2020] UKUT 278 (AAC), paragraph 84

individually and in the context of the other factors and then decide whether there was a balance between the means and the ends". The weight to place on any individual factor is a fact-sensitive matter of judgment for the specialist FTT in each case. No one factor should be placed in a *"pecking order"* or given a *"predetermined"* weight. In particular, there was no justification for assigning a special weight to a factor in a different statutory regime, a breach of which is remediable elsewhere.

CHAPTER TEN

PROCEDURE FOR BRINGING A CLAIM

FTT procedure is primarily governed by the Tribunals, Courts and Enforcement Act 2007 ("TCEA"), *The Tribunal Procedure (First-tier Tribunal) (Health, Education and Social Care Chamber) Rules 2008* ("the FTT Rules")[321], and the Chamber President's *Practice Direction: First-Tier Tribunal Health Education and Social Care Chamber, Special Educational Needs or Disability Discrimination in Schools Cases*, dated 20 April 2021 ("the Practice Direction").

What is the FTT?

The First-tier Tribunal ("FTT") was established in 2008 pursuant to the Tribunals, Courts and Enforcement Act 2007. The FTT consists of seven Chambers, including the Health, Education and Social Care Chamber ("HESC"). HESC is divided into a number of specialisms, including the First-tier Tribunal (SEND), which hears claims of disability discrimination in schools in England and appeals against decisions of local authorities in England regarding special educational needs and provision.

Prior to the establishment of the FTT in 2008, claims for disability discrimination in schools in England were heard by the Special Educational Needs and Disability Tribunal ("SENDIST"), which itself

[321] Made under section 22 and Schedule 5 of the Tribunals, Courts and Enforcement Act 2007

was established in 2002[322]. There has therefore been a specialist tribunal to consider claims for disability discrimination in schools in England for over twenty years.

The FTT is designed to operate in a less formal and more flexible manner than other jurisdictions (such as, for example, the County Court), and seeks to be accessible to non-legally represented parties. It has an inquisitorial approach to identifying the issues, obtaining relevant evidence, and questioning witnesses: an approach which has been described as less likely to undermine good relations between the parties than a more formal adversarial procedure[323].

Who can bring a claim in the FTT?

A claim for disability discrimination against a responsible body may be made to the FTT by the child's parent, or, if over compulsory school age, by the young person themselves[324]. Broadly speaking, a pupil begins to be of compulsory school age on the first day of the school term after he or she turn fives, and ceases to be of compulsory school age at the end of the academic year in which he or she turns sixteen[325]. A parent includes anyone who has parental responsibility for the child, or who has care of the child[326].

This transfer of entitlement to bring proceedings from a child's parent to a young person aligns with the procedure for appeals under section 51 of the Children and Families Act 2014 ("CFA"). However, the two

---

322 By the Special Educational Needs and Disability Act 2001

323 *R (on the application of AA) v Secretary of State for Education* [2022] EWHC 1613 (Admin), paragraph 119

324 Paragraph 3, Part 2, Schedule 17 EqA

325 Section 8 Education Act 1996; Education (Start of Compulsory School Age) Order 1998; Education (School Leaving Date) Order 1997

326 Section 212(1) EqA and section 576 Education Act 1996

statutory frameworks diverge in terms of their treatment of claimants who lack capacity[327]. Capacity is defined in section 2 of the Mental Capacity Act 2005.

The CFA and associated regulations[328] make provision for appeals under section 51 CFA to be brought by an alternative person[329] (usually the young person's parent), where the young person lacks capacity. The EqA contains no such provision. As such, where a young person lacks capacity to bring or to conduct a claim under the EqA, then it will be necessary for a litigation friend to be appointed.

The FTT Rules make no express provision about capacity or the appointment of litigation friends. However, the case law makes clear that even where a tribunal's rules do not expressly empower it to appoint litigation friends, that tribunal will nonetheless be empowered to do so in order to ensure that the incapacitated party can participate in the proceedings, in accordance with common law procedural fairness and Article 6 ECHR[330].

The issue of a claimant's capacity may be identified by the responsible body, by the claimant's legal representatives, or by the FTT. The threshold at which the FTT will be expected to pause proceedings in order to make an assessment of the claimant's capacity is likely to be where *"there is good cause for concern"* about the claimant's capacity to litigate[331]. Once brought to the FTT's attention, the FTT has broad case management powers to investigate and deal with the issue as a

327 As defined by section 2 of the Mental Capacity Act 2005

328 Special Educational Needs and Disability Regulations 2014

329 Regulation 64 Special Educational Needs and Disability Regulations 2014

330 *MM (as alternative person for C) v Royal Borough of Greenwich* [2024] UKUT 179 (AAC), paragraph 34

331 *MM (as alternative person for C) v Royal Borough of Greenwich* [2024] UKUT 179 (AAC), paragraph 33

preliminary matter, including by seeking relevant evidence from the parties[332].

It is common for parents and young people to act as litigants in person in the FTT. Parents and young people may appoint a non-legally qualified representative[333], or may receive informal emotional or practical support (for example from a friend or family member). The FTT should be notified in advance of the attendance of such a supporter at the hearing.

What is the time limit for bringing a claim?

Proceedings on a claim may not be brought after the end of the period of **6 months** starting with the date when the conduct complained of occurred[334]. The following rules apply for the purposes of determining the date on which conduct occurred[335]:

- If the contravention is attributable to a term in a contract, the conduct is to be treated as extending throughout the duration of the contract.
- Conduct extending over a period is to be treated as occurring at the end of the period.
- A failure to do something is to be treated as occurring when the person in question decided not to do it. In the absence of evidence to the contrary, a person is to be taken to decide not to do something when that person acts inconsistently with doing it, or, if that person does not act inconsistently, on the expiry of the

---

332 *Buckinghamshire County Council v SJ* [2016] UKUT 254 (AAC), paragraph 11

333 Rule 11(1) FTT Rules

334 Paragraph 4(1), Part 2, Schedule 17 EqA

335 Paragraph 4(5), Part 2, Schedule 17 EqA

period in which that person might reasonably have been expected to do it[336].

Calculation of time

Whilst the deadline for bringing a special educational needs case under section 51 CFA is extended where it would otherwise expire between 25 December and 1 January or on any day in August[337], it is important to note that the deadline for bringing a disability discrimination claim remains the same, regardless of whether the final day lands on a school holiday or not[338].

Conduct extending over a period

A common scenario is for a claimant in a disability discrimination claim to complain about a number of matters going back in time, and for one or more of the earlier matters to have occurred more than 6 months before the claim was brought (such as, for example, a series of fixed-term suspensions). In such cases, it is necessary to consider whether those earlier matters are related, such that they constitute *"conduct extending over a period"*. In order to demonstrate "*conduct extending over a period*", it is not necessary to establish a discriminatory policy, practice, scheme or regime (although such a policy, practice, scheme or regime may constitute conduct extending over a period depending on the circumstances[339]). Instead, the focus should be on:

---

336 Paragraph 4(6), Part 2, Schedule 17 EqA

337 Rule 12(3)(a) FTT Rules

338 Rule 12(3A) FTT Rules; see also *JL v Cherry Lane Primary School Governing Body* [2019] UKUT 223 (AAC) which deals with an earlier version of the FTT Rules, now amended by *The Tribunal Procedure (Amendment) Rules 2020*

339 *Barclays Bank plc v Kapur* [1991] 2 AC 355

- Whether the incidents are linked to each other, and
- Whether they are evidence of an "*ongoing situation or continuing state of affairs*"[340].

Another common scenario is for a claimant in a disability discrimination claim to complain about a matter which initially arose more than 6 months before the claim was brought, but which continues to have an impact upon the claimant (such as, for example, a decision to educate a pupil off-site). In such circumstances, it is necessary to determine whether the matter amount to "*conduct extending over a period*", or is a "*one-off act with continuing consequences*"[341]. A helpful discussion of the distinction between these two concepts can be found in the UT case of *Governing Body of School T v AA and RA*[342].

Discretion to extend time

The FTT may consider a claim which is out of time[343]. The FTT's power to extend time is discretionary, which should be exercised in the interests of justice[344]. A claimant who requires an extension of time must include a request for an extension of time and explain the reason for the delay[345]. The onus is on the claimant who requires an extension to persuade the

340 *The Governing Body of School T (Responsible Body) v AA and RR* [2023] UKUT 311 (AAC), paragraph 35

341 *The Governing Body of School T (Responsible Body) v AA and RR* [2023] UKUT 311 (AAC), paragraph 47

342 [2023] UKUT 311

343 Paragraph 4(3), Part 2, Schedule 17 EqA

344 *RD and GD v The Proprietor of Horizon Primary (SEN)* [2020] UKUT 278 (AAC), paragraph 36

345 Rule 20(4) FTT Rules

FTT to grant it[346]. On an application for an extension of time, the FTT should assess all the relevant factors, including the length of, and reasons for, the delay[347]. Other relevant facts may include:

- The extent to which the responsible body will be prejudiced by the claim being considered out of time (for example, if the delay prevents the responsible body from investigating the claim whilst the matters complained of were fresh).
- The extent to which mental ill-health or disability has impacted upon the claimant's ability to bring the claim in time[348].
- The merits of the substantive claim[349].

Paragraph 4(4), Part 2, Schedule 17 EqA creates a "*one strike*" rule which prevents repeat applications to the FTT for an extension of time. In *JL v Governing Body of Cherry Lane Primary School*[350] the UT held that a decision not to extend time made in initial case management directions, on the papers and without submissions from the parties, should not be treated as the claimant's "*one and only*" opportunity to apply for an extension of time[351]. This decision has been reflected in the updated Practice Direction, which provides that the FTT's provisional views about timeliness when considering the claim on receipt shall not be a

346 *Kumari v Greater Manchester Mental Health NHS Foundation Trust* [2022] EAT 132, paragraph 28

347 *Adedeji v University Hospitals Birmingham NHS Foundation Trust* [2021 EWCA Civ 23, paragraph 37

348 *J v K* [2019] EWCA Civ 5, paragraph 33

349 *Kumari v Greater Manchester Mental Health NHS Foundation Trust* [2022] EAT 132

350 [2019] UKUT 223 (AAC)

351 Paragraph 37

decision of the FTT for the purposes of paragraph 4(4), Part 2, Schedule 17 EqA[352].

Commencing a claim

The child's parent or young person must start proceedings by sending or delivering an application notice to the FTT so that it arrives within the relevant time limit[353]. Unlike in the County Court, there is no fee for issuing a disability discrimination claim in the FTT. There are a number of prescribed forms, available on the HM Courts and Tribunals Service website. The appropriate form depends on whether the parent or young person is seeking reinstatement following a permanent exclusion (in which case Form SEND26A or SEND26B should be used), and whether, for other types of claim, the claim is being brought by the child's parent or by the young person themselves (in which case Form SEND4A or SEND4B should be used).

The application notice must include the matters set out in rule 20(2) FTT Rules, and in paragraph 6 of the Practice Direction. This includes:

- The name and address of the claimant, and of the claimant's representative (if any).
- An address where documents for the claimant may be sent or delivered.
- The name and date of birth of the child or young person.
- The names and addresses of all persons or bodies (for example, the local authority) who have or share parental responsibility for the child or have care of the child, including an email address, if available.

---

352 Paragraph 8

353 Rule 20(1) FTT Rules

- The name and address of the responsible body or local authority (depending on the identity of the respondent), and their contact details, including an email address, if available.
- A description of the child's disability, including evidence of a medical or other professional diagnosis, if available.
- If the child or young person has an EHCP, a copy of that EHCP and appendices, if available.
- Details of the alleged discrimination, including the date or dates on which the discrimination is alleged to have taken place.
- If any part of the alleged discrimination took place outside of the time limit for bringing a claim, either:
    - An explanation of why each act of alleged discrimination should be treated as part of a course of conduct extending over a period and which other acts are said to form part of the conduct, or
    - The reasons why the FTT should, in its discretion, admit claims about alleged discrimination which occurred outside of the time limit.
- The grounds on which the claimant relies. In particular, if the claim includes an allegation of failure to make reasonable adjustments:
    - The provision, criterion or practice applied to pupils generally which placed disabled pupils, including the relevant child or young person, at a substantial disadvantage, and
    - A description of the substantial disadvantage the child or young person suffered (or would have suffered) by having the identified provision, criterion or practice applied to them.
- The result or remedy the claimant is seeking.

Registration of a claim

Application notices are considered by the FTT on receipt. In particular, the FTT:

- Considers whether the claim complies with rule 20 FTT Rules and the Practice Direction,
- Identifies the general grounds of claim to which the respondent must respond, and
- Makes initial case management directions on the papers.

The initial case management directions order will generally set a time limit for applying to vary any of the directions contained within it. If the claimant does not consider that the grounds of claim identified by the FTT properly reflect his or her complaint, then the claimant may apply for the order to be varied, within the relevant time limit. As such, it is sensible for a claimant to review the initial case management directions order carefully on receipt, to ensure that his or her complaint is fully captured.

If the FTT's provisional view on registration is that the claim (or part of it) has no reasonable prospect of success, then it may warn the claimant that it is considering exercising its discretion under rule 8(4)(c) FTT Rules to strike out all or part of the claim, and may require the claimant to provide additional information before deciding whether to do so[354].

If the FTT's provisional view is that a claim is out of time, then it may exercise its discretion to admit the claim out of time. In this case, the question of timeliness may be revisited by the FTT at the final hearing following the conclusion of the evidence. Alternatively, the FTT may refuse to admit the claim out of time. In this case, it must list the matter

[354] Paragraph 7(c) Practice Direction

for a preliminary hearing for determination of the question of timeliness[355].

Responding to a claim

The responsible body must send or deliver its response to the FTT so that it is received:

- In a claim that includes a claim for the reinstatement of the pupil following a permanent exclusion, within 15 working days after receipt of the application notice.
- In a claim which does not include such a claim, within 30 working days after receipt of the application notice[356].

The response must include the matters set out in rule 21(2) FTT Rules, and in paragraph 13 of the Practice Direction. This includes:

- The name and address of the respondent, and of the respondent's representative (if any), and an email address, if available.
- An address where documents for the respondent may be sent or delivered.
- Detailed grounds setting out what parts of the claim are admitted, detailed grounds setting out what parts of the claim are resisted with reasons, and details of any legal points that will be relied on at a final hearing.
- A signed and dated statement from any of the respondent's witnesses who are in their employment and on whose evidence the respondent intends to rely.

---

[355] Paragraph 8 Practice Direction

[356] Rule 21(1)(c)-(cc) FTT Rules

It is the responsible body's responsibility to send a copy of its response any accompanying documents to the claimant, at the same time as it sends it to the FTT[357].

Directions

The FTT will make standard directions within its initial case management directions order.

These will generally include a direction for the responsible body to send its response, its attendance form, and any documents it relies on, or which may be relevant, even if not relied on by the responsible body. Although there are no specific disclosure provisions within the FTT Rules, this direction may be read, in light of the overriding objective[358], as requiring the parties to make a reasonable search for documents at the outset of a claim, and to consider the necessity of disclosing any documents subsequently identified during the course of proceedings.

Categories of documents which are likely to be relevant may include: the pupil's pastoral or behaviour records; relevant correspondence with the pupil or his or her parents; relevant written policies and procedures; relevant information about the pupil's special educational needs and disabilities, including any external reports or assessments; evidence of relevant staff training; and, any documents evidencing the pupil's progress and attainment, and the school's monitoring of the same. Consideration may need to be given to redaction of third-party information (such as information about other pupils).

Other standard directions include:

- For the claimant to send its attendance form.
- For the parties to send final evidence.

---

[357] Rule 21(5) FTT Rules

[358] Rule 2 FTT Rules

- For the responsible body to prepare and send a paginated and indexed hearing bundle.
- The date of any telephone case management hearing, and the final hearing.

HMCTS has issued SEND40 *Guidance for Producing a Tribunal Bundle for the First-Tier Tribunal SEND*. This guidance stipulates the various sections into which the bundle must be divided, and the page limits for each section. All documents submitted by the claimant by the final evidence deadline must be included in the bundle, even if in excess of the page limit. However, either party wishing to rely on evidence above the page limit should make an application for permission to do so, using the SEND7 Request for Change procedure, and including an explanation as to why the additional pages are necessary. The SEND40 Guidance makes clear that a failure to comply with the deadline for production of the bundle will lead to the automatic barring of the responsible body from further participation in the proceedings, with reinstatement to be at the FTT's discretion. As such, it is key that the bundle deadline is complied with.

In general terms, where a party fails to comply with the FTT Rules or with a direction, the FTT may take such action as it considers just, including:

- Waiving the requirement;
- Requiring the failure to be remedied;
- Exercising its power to strike out the party's case;
- Referring the matter to the UT (where, broadly speaking, the FTT seeks for the UT to exercise its powers with respect to the attendance and examination of witnesses or the production and inspection of documents);
- Restricting a party's participation in the proceedings[359].

---

359 Rule 7 FTT Rules

Strike out

A claim will be **automatically** struck out (or the respondent will be automatically barred from taking further part in the proceedings) if the claimant (or respondent) fails to comply with a direction which stated that failure to comply *would* lead to strike out (also referred to as an "unless order")[360]. Further, the FTT **may** strike out a claim (or bar the respondent from taking further part in the proceedings) if the claimant (or respondent) has failed to comply with a direction which stated that failure to comply *could* lead to strike out[361].

If a claim has been struck out (or a respondent has been barred from taking further part in the proceedings) on either of the above bases, then the claimant may apply for reinstatement (or the respondent may apply for the bar to be lifted). Such an application must be made in writing and received by the FTT within 28 days after the date on which the FTT sent notification of the striking out (or barring) to the party[362]. Where the strike out (or barring) arises automatically as a result of an unless order, the time for an application to reinstate the claim (or lift the bar) will begin to run from the date on which the party was notified, as opposed to the date on which the automatic strike out took effect[363].

When deciding whether to reinstate the claim (or lift the bar), the FTT should have regard to the broad justice of the case in light of all of the circumstances, and may in particular consider:

---

360 Rule 8(2) FTT Rules

361 Rule 8(4)(a) FTT Rules

362 Rule 8(6)-(7) FTT Rules

363 *LW v Proprietor of Broughton Hall Catholic High School* [2023] UKUT 301 (AAC)

- The reason for the failure that led to the striking out of the case;
- Whether there was undue delay in applying for reinstatement; and
- Whether the other party would be prejudiced by the reinstatement[364].

Strike out may occur in a number of other scenarios. The FTT must strike out a claim if it does not have jurisdiction to hear it, and does not exercise its power to transfer the claim to the appropriate court or tribunal[365]. Further, FTT may exercise its discretion to strike out a claim (or bar a respondent from taking further part in the claim) if that party has failed to cooperate with the FTT to such an extent that the FTT cannot deal with the proceedings fairly and justly[366], and may exercise its discretion to strike out a claim where it considers there is no reasonable prospect of the claimant's case, or part of it, succeeding[367]. If one of these scenarios applies, the FTT must not strike out the claim (or bar the respondent) without first giving that party an opportunity to make representations[368].

Witnesses

Whilst there is usually no specific direction for the preparation of witness statements, it can be useful for the parties to do so. This allows the FTT to read the written evidence in advance of the hearing, and for that written evidence to stand as the witnesses' evidence in chief. This is particularly helpful where there are multiple witnesses, given that final

---

364 *LW v Proprietor of Broughton Hall Catholic High School* [2023] UKUT 301 (AAC), paragraphs 19–20

365 Rule 8(3) FTT Rules

366 Rule 8(4)(b) FTT Rules

367 Rule 8(4)(c) FTT Rules

368 Rule 8(5) FTT Rules

hearings are generally listed for only one day. There is no requirement in the FTT Rules for a witness statement to be verified by a statement of truth; however, it is open to witnesses to include such a statement if they wish.

The FTT generally allows a maximum of five witnesses per party. If a party wishes to call additional witnesses, he or she must make application for permission to do so, using the SEND7 Request for Change procedure.

Witnesses do not generally give their evidence on oath, but may request to (or be required to by the FTT)[369].

In the event that a witness will be abroad at the time of the final hearing, the *Presidential Guidance on Taking Evidence from Abroad* should be followed.

Applications

A party who wishes to apply for further directions, or to vary the directions already made by the FTT (for example, to extend the deadline for final evidence, to call an additional witness, or for an observer to attend the hearing) should do so using the SEND7 Request for Change Form. The party seeking the direction should generally consult the other party, and include that party's response in the SEND7 Request for Change Form.

Final hearing

As a general rule, the FTT must hold a hearing before making a decision which disposes of proceedings unless each party has consented to the matter being decided without a hearing, and the FTT considers that it is

[369] Rule 15(3) FTT Rules

able to decide the matter without a hearing[370]. The hearing must be one in which each parties' submissions and evidence are considered, as opposed to a procedural hearing[371].

Hearings must be held in private, unless the FTT considers that it is in the interests of justice for a hearing to be held in public[372]. As a general rule, the parties and the child who is the subject of the claim are entitled to attend the hearing[373], along with the parties' representatives and witnesses, the child's parent (if not a party to the claim), and any other person a party has informed the FTT they wish to attend (unless the FTT has determined that such a person should not attend)[374]. However, the FTT may determine who is permitted to attend the hearing or part of it, and may give a direction excluding from the hearing or part of it:

- Any person whose conduct the FTT considers is disrupting or is likely to disrupt the hearing.
- Any person whose presence the FTT considers is likely to prevent another person from giving evidence or making submissions freely.
- Any person who the FTT considers should be excluded in order to give effect to a direction under rule 14(2) FTT Rules (withholding information likely to cause harm).
- Any person where the purpose of the hearing would be defeated by the attendance of that person.

---

370 Rule 23(1) FTT Rules

371 *AB v The Governing Body of Kingston Grammar School* [2024] UKUT 406 (AAC)

372 Rule 26(2) FTT Rules

373 Rule 24 FTT Rules

374 Practice Direction, paragraph 20

- The relevant child or young person, if the FTT considers that his or her presence at the hearing would be adverse to their interests[375].

The FTT may give a direction excluding a witness from a hearing until that witness gives evidence[376]. However, this provision is not commonly used in practice, and it is more usual for all witnesses to attend the hearing from the outset.

If a party fails to attend the hearing, the FTT may proceed with the hearing if satisfied that the party has been notified of the hearing (or that reasonable steps have been taken to do so), and that it is in the interests of justice for the hearing to proceed[377].

Final hearings generally take place remotely via video link. However, when considering the arrangements for the final hearing, the FTT must consider whether any measures are necessary to ensure, so far as practicable, that the parties are able to participate fully in the proceedings in accordance with the overriding objective[378], and to give effect to the *Senior President of Tribunals' October 2008 Practice Direction: First tier and Upper Tribunal Child, Vulnerable Adult and Sensitive Witnesses*[379]. This may, in certain circumstances, include consideration of the need for an in-person hearing[380].

---

375 Rule 26(4)-(5) FTT Rules

376 Rule 26(6) FTT Rules

377 Rule 27 FTT Rules

378 Rule 2 FTT Rules

379 See for example *AA and BA v A Local Authority (SEN)* [2021] UKUT 54 (AAC) and *TS and SM v Liverpool City Council* [2024] UKUT 201 (AAC)

380 *TC and BW v London Borough of Islington (SEN)* [2021] UKUT 196, paragraph 7

Final hearings should be conducted by a panel, consisting of one legally qualified judge, and either one or two non-legally qualified specialist members (depending on whether the case has been designated by a judge as complex). Where there is clear disagreement (other than in respect of a matter of law) between a judge and a member sitting as a two-person panel, then the judge must direct a hearing before a newly appointed three-person panel[381].

The FTT is a specialist and inquisitorial tribunal, and panel members may use their own expertise to decide an issue. However, where panel members rely upon their own knowledge without giving the parties an opportunity to comment, this may constitute a breach of natural justice[382].

The FTT may give a decision orally at a hearing[383], but does not generally do so; instead, it sends a written decision to the parties, usually within 10 working days. The FTT must provide reasons for a final decision[384]. In June 2024, the Senior President of Tribunals issued guidance on the giving of written reasons for decisions in the FTT[385], stating that reasons must be *"adequate, clear, appropriately concise, and focused upon the principal controversial issues on which the outcome of the case has turned"*.

---

381 Practice Direction: Panel Composition in the First-tier Tribunal, Health, Education and Social Care (HESC) Chamber, dated 30 December 2024, made pursuant to the First-tier Tribunal and Upper Tribunal (Composition of Tribunal) Order 2008.

382 *Harrow Council v AM* [2013] UKUT 157 (AAC), paragraph 35

383 Rule 30(1) FTT Rules

384 Rule 30(2) FTT Rules

385 2024 WL 03471204

Confidentiality

The FTT is empowered to make an order prohibiting the disclosure or publication of either (a) specified documents or information relating to the proceedings; or (b) any matter likely to lead members of the public to identify any person whom the FTT considers should not be identified[386]. In practice, the FTT will generally make an order in the latter terms at the outset of proceedings. Further, depending on the circumstances of the case, disclosure to third parties of information relating to proceedings may constitute a contempt of court pursuant to section 12 of the Administration of Justice Act 1960[387]. As such, where a party wishes to disclose information arising out of proceedings to a third party (such as Ofsted, the Independent Schools Inspectorate ("ISI") or the Equality and Human Rights Commission ("EHRC")), then it will be generally be necessary to seek the FTT's permission to do so.

The FTT Procedure Rules also make provision for a form of "closed material" procedure[388], whereby one party may seek permission to withhold disclosure of a document or information from another party, in circumstances where such disclosure would be likely to cause the latter party or some other person serious harm, and where the FTT is satisfied, having regards to the interests of justice, that such a step is proportionate.

Settlement

As part of their duty to help the FTT to further the overriding objective and to cooperate with the FTT[389], parties are encouraged to explore

---

[386] Rule 14(1) FTT Rules

[387] See *Presidential Guidance: Recording of Hearings and Transcription of Recordings in* HESC, 18 December 2023, paragraphs 41 – 42; cf *ML v Tonbridge Grammar School* [2012] UKUT 283 (AAC), paragraph 27

[388] Rule 14(2) – (7) FTT Rules

[389] Rule 2(4) FTT Rules

whether they can settle their claim before the final hearing. Depending on the remedies sought by the claimant, such a settlement could include the offer of an apology (potentially without admission of liability), an agreement for staff training, or an adjustment to school practices or policies. Where the parties are able to reach agreement, the claimant may agree to seek permission to withdraw his or her claim[390], or the parties may request the FTT to make a consent order disposing of the proceedings[391]. The FTT may only make a consent order where it considers it appropriate to do so.

Costs

The usual rule in the FTT is that each party pays his or her own legal costs. The UT has observed that *"there are good and obvious reasons for the rule. Tribunal proceedings should be as brief, straightforward and informal as possible. And it is crucial that parties should not be deterred from bringing or defending appeals through fear of an application for costs"*[392].

Nonetheless, the FTT is empowered to order a party to pay another's party's legal costs in the following two scenarios:

- There are "wasted costs" (that is, costs incurred as a result of an improper, unreasonable or negligent act or omission by a legal or other representative); or,
- A party or his or her representative has acted unreasonably in bringing, defending or conducting the proceedings[393].

An order for costs should be *"the exception rather than the rule"*, and

[390] Rule 17 FTT Rules

[391] Rule 29(1) FTT Rules

[392] *MG v Cambridgeshire County Council* [2017] UKUT 172 (AAC), paragraph 26

[393] Rule 10(1) FTT Rules

should be made *"only in the most obvious cases"*[394]. When considering whether to make a costs order on account of unreasonable conduct, the FTT should ask:

- Whether the party acted unreasonably in bringing, defending or conducting the proceedings;
- If he or she did, whether the FTT should make an order for costs;
- If so, in what amount.

The case law suggests that conduct cannot be described as unreasonable simply because it leads in the event to an unsuccessful result or because other more cautious legal representatives would have acted differently. Instead, the *"acid test is whether the conduct permits of a reasonable explanation"*[395]. Whilst the assessment of whether a party has acted unreasonably is an objective question of fact, the second and third limbs of the test allow for the exercise of a broad discretion[396].

The FTT may make a costs order on its own initiative, or on an application by a party. A party wishing to apply for costs must do so no later than 14 days after the date on which the FTT sends a decision notice recording the decision which finally disposes of all issues in the proceedings, or a notice that the withdrawal of the proceedings has taken effect[397]. The "decision notice" in question is the substantive decision on the claim, and not the determination of any application for permission to appeal[398]. The UT has indicated that applications for costs should be

394 *MG v Cambridgeshire County Council* [2017] UKUT 172 (AAC), paragraph 27

395 *Ridehalgh v Horsefield* [1994] Ch. 205, as applied in *NS and RS v Kent County Council* [2021] UKUT 311 (AAC)

396 *MG v Cambridgeshire County Council* [2017] UKUT 172 (AAC), paragraphs 29 – 30

397 Rule 10(40 – (5) FTT Rules

398 *KM v Cheshire West and Chester Council* [2024] UKUT 89 (AAC)

"pithy, succinct and focussed" and that the *"basis of the application should be clearly set out at the outset"*[399].

[399] *NS and RS v Kent County Council* [2021] UKUT 311 (AAC), paragraph 149

CHAPTER ELEVEN

REMEDIES

If the FTT finds that a responsible body has contravened the EqA, it has a broad and flexible power to "*make such order as it thinks fit*"[400]. This power "*may, in particular, be exercised with a view to obviating or reducing the adverse effect on the person of any matter to which the claim relates*"[401]. This power should be exercised proportionately[402].

The range of remedies which the FTT is able to order is much wider than the County Court and Employment Tribunal, and can include[403]:

- A declaration of disability discrimination;
- Training of or guidance for staff;
- Changes to the responsible body's policies and procedures;
- Provision of additional tuition to enable the pupil to catch up on missed learning;
- Provision of trips or opportunities to make up for any activities missed;
- Changes to the location of lessons or activities (but not changes to the physical premises);
- Admission or reinstatement of the pupil to the school;
- An apology from the responsible body to the pupil;

[400] Schedule 17, Part 2, paragraph 5(2) EqA

[401] Schedule 17, Part 2, paragraph 5(3) EqA

[402] *Gayhurst Community School v ER (SEN)* [2013] UKUT 558 (AAC), paragraph 27

[403] *ML v Tonbridge Grammar School* [2012] UKUT 283, paragraph 18

- Disclosure of the decision to any relevant external organisations (such as the Equality and Human Rights Commission ("EHRC") or Ofsted);
- Amending the school's record (for example, to remove reference to an exclusion)[404].

The FTT will generally order the responsible body to take any such steps within a specified period of time.

The FTT does **not** have the power to order the payment of compensation[405]. However, parents may in appropriate circumstances consider using an FTT finding of disability discrimination to support a companion County Court claim[406] (for example, a claim for negligence[407], or, in the case of an independent school, for breach of contract), which may in turn may lead to the responsible body being ordered to pay compensation in respect of any financial losses incurred. Further, a finding of disability discrimination may carry significant reputational risk. For example, such a finding may have implications for a school's Ofsted inspection or an independent schools' compliance with the Independent Schools Standards[408], and, in the case of schools that are

---

404 *Gayhurst Community School v ER (SEN)* [2013] UKUT 558 (AAC), paragraph 24

405 Schedule 17, Part 2, paragraph 5(3)(b) EqA

406 Subject to the relevant time limits for bringing such a claim, and subject to any requirement for permission to disclose any relevant FTT document to a third-party

407 *Phelps v London Borough of Hillingdon* [2000] UKHL 47

408 Contained in the Schedule to the Education (Independent School Standards) Regulations 2014

registered charities, may constitute a serious incident, requiring a report to the Charity Commission[409].

Although not expressly ruled out by broad wording of paragraph 5, Part 2, Schedule 17 EqA, it is generally understood that the FTT will not make an order requiring a responsible body to make physical alterations to the school premises[410], or to dismiss a particular member of staff[411].

No jurisdiction to order the payment of compensation

The FTT's lack of power to award damages contrasts with the County Court's power to do so in further or higher education disability discrimination claims, and in schools discrimination claims on the grounds of other protected characteristics. In *R (on the application of AA) v Secretary of State for Education*[412], the High Court held that this difference in treatment did **not** constitute a breach of Article 14 of the European Convention on Human Rights ("ECHR")[413] taken with Article 1 of Protocol 1[414], Article 2 of Protocol 1[415], or Article 8[416].

The High Court concluded that this difference did not constitute unfavourable treatment, and that there were in fact substantial benefits to bringing a claim in the FTT. In particular, "*there are no court fees or*

---

409 See the Charity Commission's June 2014 *Guidance: How to report a serious incident in your charity*

410 See *SEND4: How to claim against disability discrimination in schools – a guide for parents*

411 See *www.ipsea.org.uk/disability-discrimination*

412 [2022] EWHC 1613 (Admin)

413 Right to non-discrimination in the enjoyment of human rights

414 Protection of property

415 Right to education

416 Right to respect for private and family life

formal pleading requirements; the procedure is designed to be less adversarial and more flexible, informal and inquisitorial; there is the benefit of specialist judges who have experience and knowledge of disability issues; and the range of remedies available is far wider (being designed to put the child's education back on track)"[417]. Further, the High Court held that, to the extent that the difference did constitute unfavourable treatment, such treatment was justified, on the basis that it prioritised effective educational remedies, and discouraged the development of a culture of litigation[418].

Although a question on the effectiveness of the current remedies available to the FTT was included in the SEND Review consultation Green Paper published by the former Conservative government in March 2022, the then Secretary of State for Education confirmed in *R (on the application of CU) v Secretary of State for Education*)[419] that this was an information gathering exercise, and that there were no proposals to expand the FTT's powers in this respect[420].

Reinstatement

The UT case of *Proprietor of Ashdown House School v JKL*[421] confirmed that the FTT is empowered to order the reinstatement of a permanently excluded pupil to an independent school further to a finding of disability discrimination. The UT confirmed that, when considering whether to exercise its discretion to make such an order, the FTT should bear in mind the principles relevant to orders for specific performance of a contract involving personal service, including:

---

417 Paragraph 77

418 Paragraphs 123 – 127

419 [2024] EWHC 638 (Admin)

420 Paragraph 28

421 [2019] UKUT 259 (AAC)

- whether trust and confidence has broken down, or whether a continued relationship is unworkable for some other reason; and,
- whether the order requires specific performance of continuous duties, the due performance of which might require constant supervision by the court[422].

The UT held that the order for reinstatement was an order *"to achieve a result"* rather than an order to *"carry on an activity for a period of time"*, and therefore did not fall foul of the prohibition on ordering specific performance of arrangements requiring constant supervision[423]. Further, the UT observed that, when drawing up an order, the FTT must
"be careful not to impose obligations which cannot be precisely drawn lest they be insufficiently precise to be capable of being specifically performed and thus insufficiently precise to found an order for committal"[424].

The FTT does **not** have the power to stay the decision of a responsible body to permanently exclude a pupil pending the final hearing of a claim for disability discrimination[425]. A claimant seeking such an interim order would instead have consider the appropriateness of seeking an interim mandatory injunction, either within the context of an application for judicial review, or, in the case of a private independent school, a claim for breach of contract[426].

---

422 Paragraphs 214 – 222

423 Paragraph 237

424 Paragraph 239

425 *DB v Academy Transformation Trust (SEND)* [2022] UKUT 66 (AAC)

426 See *Proprietor of Ashdown School v JKL* [2019] UKUT 259 (AAC), paragraph 192; see also *Ross v Stanbridge Earls School* [2002] EWHC 2255 (QB), paragraph 15

Apologies

The FTT is empowered to order the responsible body to issue an apology to the child, or to his or her parents.

In *ML v Tonbridge Grammar School*[427], the UT held that an order for an apology may have a wider purpose than merely preventing further discrimination against the child in question. The UT observed that *"To the extent that an apology is an acceptance that an act or omission has been unlawful, an order that a school apologise can be regarded as part of the vindication of the claimant. To the extent that an apology is also an assurance as to future conduct, an order that there be an apology gives teeth to the declaration".*[428]

However, in *Gayhurst Community School v ER (SEN)*[429], the UT appeared to narrow down the circumstances in which it may be appropriate to order a responsible body to issue an apology. The UT noted that an apology made under compulsion *"merely creates resentment on one side and at best an illusion on the other. It does nothing for the parties' future relations and may even make them worse"*[430]. The UT held that the FTT *"should always satisfy itself, before ordering an apology, that it will be of some true value"*[431].

---

[427] [2012] UKUT 283 (AAC)

[428] Paragraph 22

[429] [2013] UKUT 558 (AAC)

[430] Paragraph 25

[431] Paragraph 26

More recently, these conflicting authorities were considered by the UT in *Proprietor of Ashdown School v JKL*[432], and the following helpful guidance was handed down[433]:

- An apology may have a wider purpose than merely preventing further discrimination against the child in question. To the extent that an apology is an assurance as to future conduct, an order that there be an apology gives teeth to a declaration of unlawful discrimination;
- There can be value in an apology: apologies are very important to many people and may provide solace for the emotional or psychological harm caused by unlawful conduct. An apology might reduce the mental distress, hurt and indignity associated with a permanent exclusion. It might also assist with recovery, forgiveness and reconciliation. An order that there be an apology can be regarded as part of the vindication of the claimant;
- The FTT should consider whether the apology should more appropriately be made to the child or to his parents. In the case of very young children the latter may be more appropriate for obvious reasons;
- An order to make an apology may well be appropriate when there is already an acceptance that there has been discrimination or unlawful conduct or where there is an acceptance and an acknowledgment of the FTT's findings on responsibility;
- However, the fact that there has been a contested hearing and that the respondent has strenuously disputed that there has been any discrimination or unlawful conduct is not decisive against ordering an apology;
- Nevertheless, particularly where there has been a dispute or a contested hearing, the FTT should always consider whether it is appropriate to make an order and bear in mind that it may create

432 [2019] UKUT 259 (AAC)

433 Paragraph 256

resentment on one side and an illusion on the other, do nothing for future relations and may make them even worse;

- Before ordering an apology, a tribunal should always satisfy itself that it will be of some true value;
- The FTT should always be aware that there may be problems of supervision if it accepts responsibility for overseeing the terms of the apology which can result in drawn out arguments over wording.

Enforcing an order of the FTT

In the vast majority of cases, responsible bodies comply with orders of the FTT, and it is unnecessary for claimants to take steps to enforce the same. However, where enforcement is required, it is important to note that, unlike the County Court, the FTT does not have enforcement powers of its own[434]. Instead, depending on the circumstances, it may be possible to enforce an FTT order:

- By invoking the inherent jurisdiction of the High Court to assist the FTT in the exercise of its jurisdiction[435];
- By applying to the High Court for committal for contempt[436];
- By seeking a direction from the Secretary of State (in respect of a maintained school or non-maintained special school), or by

[434] Explanatory notes to the Tribunals, Courts and Enforcement Act 2007, paragraph 32

[435] *Proprietor of Ashdown House school v JKL* [2019] UKUT 259 (AAC), paragraph 120 – 136

[436] *Proprietor of Ashdown House school v JKL* [2019] UKUT 259 (AAC), paragraph 137 – 168

requesting the Secretary of State to enforce obligations under a funding agreement (in respect of an Academy)[437];

- By way of an application for an injunction brought by the Equality and Human Rights Commission ("EHRC") under section 24 of the Equality Act 2006[438];
- By way of judicial review (in the case of a maintained school but not in the case of an independent school, which is not a "public body" and is therefore not amenable to judicial review)[439].

---

437 Sections 496 – 497 of the Education Act 1996, as applied by section 87 EqA; see also *ML v Tonbridge Grammar School* [2012] UKUT 283 (AAC), paragraph 26

438 *Proprietor of Ashdown House school v JKL* [2019] UKUT 259 (AAC), paragraph 169 – 178

439 *Proprietor of Ashdown House school v JKL* [2019] UKUT 259 (AAC), paragraph 179 – 198

CHAPTER TWELVE

CHALLENGING AN FTT DECISION

The FTT is empowered to amend, review and set aside its decisions in certain circumstances. Further, FTT decisions (other than the excluded decisions identified in section 11 TCEA) are amenable to appeal to the UT on a point of law. The rules governing reviews and appeals are set out in the Tribunals, Courts and Enforcement Act 2007 ("the TCEA"), the *Tribunal Procedure (First-tier Tribunal) (Health, Education and Social Care Chamber) Rules 2008* ("the FTT Rules"), and the *Tribunal Procedure (Upper Tribunal) Rules 2008* ("the UT Rules").

The FTT may treat an application for a decision to be amended, set aside or reviewed, or for permission to appeal against a decision, as an application for any other one of those things[440].

Challenging a case management decision

Rule 6(5) FTT Rules permits a party, or any other person given notice of a direction made by the FTT, to apply for another direction which amends, suspends or sets aside the first direction. Any such application should be made using the SEND7 Request for Change Form. A decision to refuse to review a direction further to an application under rule 6(5) FTT is not an excluded decision for the purposes of section 11 TCEA, and is therefore amenable to appeal[441].

---

440 Rule 50 FTT Rules

441 *LM v London Borough of Lewisham* [2009] UKUT 204 (AAC), paragraph 14

Correcting errors and setting aside decisions on procedural grounds

Paragraph 15, Part 1, Schedule 5 TCEA provides for rules for the correction of accidental errors in a decision or record of a decision, and for the setting aside of a decision on the grounds of procedural irregularity. These rules are rule 44 FTT Rules ("clerical mistakes and accidental slips or omissions") and rule 45 FTT rules ("setting aside a decision which disposes of proceedings").

Rule 44 FTT Rules: the slip rule

The "slip rule" in rule 44 FTT Rules provides that the FTT may *"at any time correct any clerical mistake or other accidental slip or omission in a decision, direction or any document produced by it"*[442]. The FTT may do so of its own initiative, by sending notification of the amendment to the parties. Alternatively, either party may apply for a correction using the SEND7 Request for Change Form. The slip rule should only be used to bring a decision into line with what the FTT actually decided (as opposed to making substantive changes based on what the FTT should have decided)[443].

Rule 45 FTT Rules: setting aside a decision on procedural grounds

The FTT may set aside a decision which disposes of the proceedings, or part of such a decision, and re-make the decision or relevant part of it, if:

- There has been a procedural irregularity in the proceedings (including, but not limited to, a document relating to the proceedings not having been sent or received at an appropriate time by a party or a party's representative, a document relating to the proceedings not having been sent to the FTT at an

---

[442] Rule 44 FTT Rules

[443] *London Borough of Camden v KT* [2023] UKUT 225 (AAC), paragraph 14

appropriate time, or the non-attendance of a party or a party's representative at a hearing), and

- The FTT considers it in the interests of justice to do so[444].

An application for a decision (or part of a decision) to be set aside on this basis must be made by a party in writing (using the SEND20C application form) so that it is received no later than 28 days after the date on which the FTT sent notice of the decision to the party[445]. Although not expressly stated within rule 45 FTT Rules, the FTT is likely to have power to extend the time limit[446].

The power to set aside on procedural grounds is limited to "*procedural mishaps and errors*", and does not allow a decision to be set aside for matters that relate to the substance of the decision[447]. The power to set aside on procedural grounds is exercised pursuant to paragraph 15, Part 1, Schedule 5 TCEA, and not pursuant to section 9 TCEA. As such, a decision to set aside on this basis does not constitute an excluded decision for the purpose of section 11 TCEA (and is therefore amenable to review or appeal)[448].

Reviews

Section 9 TCEA empowers the FTT to review a decision (other than the excluded decisions identified in section 11 TCEA) subject to any limitations provided for by tribunal procedure rules. The term "decision"

---

444 Rule 45 FTT Rules

445 Rule 45(3) FTT Rules

446 Rule 5(3)(a) FTT Rules

447 *Worcestershire County Council v JJ* [2014] UKUT 406 (AAC), paragraph 12

448 *Worcestershire County Council v JJ* [2014] UKUT 406 (AAC), paragraphs 19 – 23

should be read broadly[449], and can include a strike out following an unless order (pursuant to rule 8 FTT Rules), a consent to withdrawal (pursuant to rule 17 FTT Rules), and the making of a consent order (pursuant to rule 29 FTT Rules)[450].

The FTT Rules provide for a review to take place in just two circumstances:

- Following receipt of an application for permission to appeal (pursuant to rule 47 FTT Rules); and,
- In a special educational needs case where the circumstances relevant to the decision have changed (pursuant to rule 48 FTT Rules).

The latter circumstance is unique to SEN cases brought under section 51 of the Children and Families Act 2014, and is therefore not relevant for the purposes of this book.

On receiving an application for permission to appeal, the FTT must first consider whether to review the decision. The FTT may only review the decision if it is satisfied that there has been an error of law[451]. The power to review a decision is discretionary, and has a primary purpose of avoiding an unnecessary appeal where the FTT has made an obvious error of law, to enable appropriate corrective action to be taken without delay[452]. This power is not designed to usurp the UT's function of

449 *LS v London Borough of Lambeth (HB)* [2010] UKUT 461 (AAC), paragraph 90

450 *R v FTT and Hertfordshire County Council* [2012] UKUT 213 (AAC), paragraph 24; see also *London Borough of Camden v FG (SEN)* [2010] UKUT 249 (AAC), paragraph 30

451 Rule 49(1)(a) FTT Rules

452 *B v Worcestershire County Council (SEN)* [2010] UKUT 292 (AAC), paragraph 8; *R (RB) v First-tier Tribunal (Review)* [2010] UKUT 160 (AAC), paragraphs 22 – 29

determining appeals on contentious points of law, or to enable a different FTT panel to take a different view, where both views are tenable[453].

The FTT may only consider reviewing a decision in a disability discrimination claim upon receipt of an application for permission to appeal. As such, it is not open to a party to such a claim to make a freestanding application for a review under rules 47 FTT Rules (although that party may expressly invite the FTT to consider the same within an application for permission to appeal).

On review, the FTT may:

- correct accidental errors in the decision,
- amend reasons given for the decision, or
- set aside the decision[454].

The FTT must notify the parties in writing of the outcome of the review, and of any right of appeal in relation to the outcome[455]. If the FTT takes any action in relation to a decision following a review without first giving every party an opportunity to make representations, then the notification must state that any party that did not have an opportunity to make representations may apply for such action to be set aside and for the decision to be reviewed again[456].

The FTT can review a decision only once. Once the FTT has decided not to review a decision, it cannot then change its mind and decide to conduct a review[457]. Where the FTT, having reviewed a decision, sets

---

453 *R (RB) v First-tier Tribunal (Review)* [2010] UKUT 160 (AAC), paragraphs 22 – 29; explanatory notes to the TCEA, paragraph 100

454 Section 9(4) TCEA

455 Rule 49(2) FTT Rules

456 Rule 49(3) FTT Rules

457 Section 9(10) TCEA

that decision aside and re-makes it, the latter, re-made decision should be treated as a fresh decision[458].

Where the FTT sets aside a decision, it must either re-decide the matter itself, or refer the matter to the UT, for the UT to decide[459]. When deciding which option to take, the FTT should consider whether the matter would benefit from the practical educational expertise of the lay members of the FTT[460], and whether it may be desirable for further factual findings to be made by the FTT[461]. If the FTT opts to re-decide the matter itself, it should generally hold an oral hearing unless the parties are content to proceed by way of written submissions alone[462].

When re-deciding a matter following a set aside, the FTT or UT (as the case may be) may make such findings of fact as it considers appropriate[463].

There has previously been conflicting case law as to whether a discrete part of a decision may be reviewed and / or set aside (as opposed to the

---

458 Section 9(11) TCEA; *Essex County Council v TB (SEN)* [2014] UKUT 559 (AAC), paragraph 46

459 Section 9(5) – (6) TCEA

460 *Harrow Council v AM* [2013] UKUT 157 (AAC), paragraph 18

461 *R (RB) v First-tier Tribunal (Review)* [2010] UKUT 160 (AAC), paragraph 28

462 *Essex County Council v TB (SEN)* [2014] UKUT 559 (AAC), paragraph 45; by application of the equivalent UT rule (that is, rule 34 of the *Tribunal Procedure (Upper Tribunal) Rules 2008*), it might be expected that the UT, if re-deciding the matter, should have regard to any view expressed by a party when deciding whether to hold a hearing.

463 Section 9(8) TCEA

whole)[464]. This conflict was resolved by the Court of Appeal case of *Point West GR Ltd v Bassi*[465], which held (in the context of a case originating in the FTT (Property Chamber)) that the FTT has a discretion to narrow the scope of a review to only part of a decision. The decision in *Point West GR Ltd v Bassi* was subsequently applied in the context of the FTT (Health, Education and Social Care) by *Westminster City Council v First Tier Tribunal*[466].

Appeals

The UT is empowered to hear appeals by parties against decisions of the FTT[467], on a point of law. Appeals from decisions of the FTT are heard by the UT (Administrative Appeals Chamber ("AAC")). There is no automatic right to appeal, and a party who wishes to do so must apply for permission[468].

Application for permission to the FTT

A party wishing to appeal must first apply for permission from the FTT[469]. The application must be made on Form SEND20A, and must identify the decision being challenged, the alleged error(s) of law, and the result sought by the appellant[470]. The application for permission must be

---

464 See *Harrow Council v AM* [2013] UKUT 157 (AAC), paragraph 18, and *Essex County Council v TB (SEN)* [2014] UKUT 559 (AAC), paragraph 43

465 [2020] EWCA Civ 795

466 *Westminster City Council v First Tier Tribunal* [2023] UKUT 177 (AAC)

467 Section 11 TCEA

468 Section 11(3) TCEA

469 Rule 21(2) UT Rules; Rule 46 FTT Rules

470 Rule 46(5) FTT Rules

delivered to the FTT so that it is received no later than **28 days** after the latest of the dates that the FTT sends the following:

- The decision notice.
- The written reasons for the decision, if the decision disposes of all issues in the proceedings, or disposes of a preliminary issue[471].
- Notification of amended reasons for, or correction of, the decision following a review.
- Notification that an application for the decision to be set aside has been unsuccessful[472].

The FTT is empowered to extend the time limit if the application is made out of time. An out-of-time application must include a request for an extension of time, and must explain the reason for the delay[473].

If the FTT refuses permission to appeal, or gives permission to appeal on limited grounds, then it must send to the parties a statement of its reasons for refusal of permission (or of refusal of permission on one or more of the pleaded grounds, as the case may be), along with notification of the right to make a further application to the UT for permission to appeal, the time limit for and method of making such an application[474].

If the FTT gives permission to appeal, then the appellant should provide a notice of appeal to the UT using Form UT4, within one month of the

---

[471] Unless the FTT directs that the time limit for appealing a decision on a preliminary issue shall run from the date of the decision that disposes of the proceedings in their entirety, pursuant to rule 46(2A) FTT Rules.

[472] Only if an application for the decision to be set aside was made within the time stipulated in rule 45 FTT Rules or any extension of that time granted by the FTT.

[473] Rule 46(4) FTT Rules

[474] Rule 47(4) FTT Rules

date of grant of permission[475]. The UT is empowered to extend the time limit if the notice of appeal is provided out of time. An out-of-time notice must include a request for an extension of time, and must explain the reason for the delay[476].

Renewed application for permission to the UT

If the FTT has refused an application for permission to appeal, has refused to admit the application (on the grounds that it has been made out of time), or has granted the application on limited grounds, then the appellant may renew the application for permission to appeal to the UT[477]. The application must be received by the UT no later than a month after the date of the FTT decision on the application for appeal[478]. The UT is empowered to extend the time limit if the application is made out of time. An out-of-time application must include a request for an extension of time, and must explain the reason for the delay[479].

The application must be made in writing, using Form UT4, and must identify the name and address of the appellant and of the appellant's representative (if relevant), an address for service of documents, the decision being challenged, the alleged error(s) of law, and whether the appellant wants the application to be dealt with at a hearing[480]. The application must append a copy of the decision being challenged, the accompanying statement of reasons (if separate), and the FTT decision on the application for permission to appeal[481]. If the FTT refused to

[475] Rule 23 UT Rules

[476] Rule 23(5) UT Rules

[477] Rule 21(2) UT Rules

[478] Rule 21(3)(b) UT Rules

[479] Rule 21(6) UT Rules

[480] Rule 21(4) UT Rules

[481] Rule 21(5) UT Rules

admit the appellant's initial application for permission to appeal on the grounds that it was out of time, then the renewed application must include the reason why the initial application was out of time, and the UT must only admit the renewed application if it considers that it is in the interests of justice to do so[482].

If the UT refuses permission to appeal, it must send written notice of the refusal, and of the reasons for the refusal, to the appellant[483]. If the UT has refused permission to appeal, refuses to admit a late application, or grants permission on limited grounds following consideration of the papers only, then the appellant may apply for the decision to be reconsidered at an oral hearing[484]. An application for an oral hearing must be made in writing, within 14 days of the UT decision.

There is no requirement for a respondent to be put on notice at the time of an application for permission to appeal. If and when permission is granted, the respondent must be notified, and may provide a response to the appeal[485].

Grounds of appeal

Appeals to the UT can only be made on the basis that there has been an error of law. As such, the function of the UT on appeal is ***"not to take the primary decision but to ensure that the primary decision-maker [in this***

---

482 Rule 21(7) UT Rules; for an example of the application of this rule, see *MS and LS v Wakefield Council* [2021] UKUT 316 (AAC), paragraph 20

483 Rule 22(1) UT Rules

484 Rule 22(4) UT Rules; unless the UT has already recorded the whole or part of an application to be totally without merit, in which case the appellant may not seek for the application (or part of the application) to be reconsidered at an oral hearing, see rule 22(4A) UT Rules

485 Rule 24 UT Rules

context, the FTT] has operated within lawful limits"[486]. An error of law can arise in many different contexts, however some common categories of error of law include[487]:

- **Misunderstanding or misapplying the law:** a failure to apply or to properly apply the relevant law. For example, in *KTS v Governing Body of a Community Primary School*[488], the UT held that the FTT had erred in law when it found that, because the responsible body had made *some* reasonable adjustments, that was sufficient to discharge its duty under section 20 EqA, notwithstanding that *further* reasonable adjustments could have been made.
- **Procedural impropriety:** a procedural irregularity capable of making a difference to the outcome or the fairness of the proceedings[489]. For example, in *Harrow Council v AM*[490], the UT held that the FTT had erred in law by relying on its own knowledge about the provision available in mainstream schools without giving the parties an opportunity to comment.
- **Inadequacy of reasons:** a failure to provide an adequate account of the facts and reasoning to enable the parties to understand why they have won or lost. For example, in *A Multi Academy Trust v RR*[491], the UT held that the FTT had erred in law by providing inadequate reasons when it made a comparison between disabled and non-disabled pupils without indicating what it meant by these terms.

---

486 *Bradley v The Jockey Club*, [2005] EWCA Civ 1056, paragraph 17

487 *R (Iran) v Secretary of State for the Home Department* [2005] EWCA Civ 982, paragraph 9

488 [2024] UKUT 139 (AAC)

489 *R (Iran) v Secretary of State for the Home Department* [2005] EWCA Civ 982, paragraph 9

490 [2013] UKUT 157 (AAC)

491 [2024] UKUT 9 (AAC)

- **Taking into account irrelevant factors / failure to take into account relevant factors:** for example, in *MW v Halton Borough Council*[492], the UT held that the FTT had erred in law by overlooking evidence of a Consultant Child and Adolescent Psychiatrist that the child, B, would benefit from a high teacher ratio in a specialist teaching environment for children with autistic spectrum disorder. It is important to distinguish between a failure to take into account relevant factors, and a disagreement as to the appropriate weight to give a relevant factor. The question of evidential weight is *"quintessentially a matter for the tribunal"* and is unlikely to be amenable to appeal[493] (unless on irrationality grounds).
- **Irrationality / perversity:** making a decision that no reasonable tribunal would reached[494]. The irrationality / perversity test sets a very high threshold. It requires the FTT's conclusion to be irrational or wholly unsupported by the evidence[495].
- **Perverse conclusion on the facts:** This might include making perverse of irrational findings on a matter or matters that were material to the outcome, failing to take into account and / or resolve conflicts of fact or opinion on material matters, or making a mistake as to a material fact which could be established by objective and uncontentious evidence, where the appellant and / or his advisors were not responsible for the mistake, and where unfairness resulting from the fact that a mistake was made[496].

---

492 [2010] UKUT 34 (AAC)

493 *R (V) v Asylum and Immigration Tribunal and others* [2009] EWHC 1902 (Admin), paragraph 36

494 *Worcestershire County Council v SE* [2020] UKUT 217 (AAC)

495 *London Borough of Islington v A Parent* [2024] UKUT 252 (AAC), paragraph 29

496 *R (Iran) v Secretary of State for the Home Department* [2005] EWCA Civ 982, paragraph 9

The case law provides some general principles for approaching an FTT decision on appeal. In particular:

- When considering an "inadequacy of reasons" challenge, the appeal should only be allowed where the UT *"really cannot understand the original judge's thought processes when he or she was making material findings"*[497]. It is not incumbent upon the FTT to set out every step in its reasoning, so long as it *"deals with such matters as are vital to [its] conclusion"* and *"explains the matter in which [it] resolved them"*[498].
- As an expert tribunal, the FTT will generally be taken to be aware of the relevant authorities within the jurisdiction being exercised, and to be applying those cases without the need to refer to them specifically, unless it is clear from the language of the decision that they have failed to do so[499].
- When considering a "failure to take into account relevant factors" challenge, the UT should be slow to infer that a relevant point has not been taken into account simply because it was not expressly mentioned by the FTT[500].

Procedure on appeal

The UT Rules give the UT a broad discretion as to the procedure on appeal, including as to whether to hold an oral hearing, or to decide the

---

[497] *HJ (Afghanistan) v Secretary of State for the Home Department* [2017] EWCA Civ 2716, paragraph 11

[498] *HJ (Afghanistan) v Secretary of State for the Home Department* [2017] EWCA Civ 2716, paragraph 14

[499] *Ullah v Secretary of State for the Home Department* [2020] EWCA Civ 201, paragraph 26, applying *AA (Nigeria) v Secretary of State for the Home Department* [2020] EWCA Civ 1296

[500] *Ullah v Secretary of State for the Home Department* [2020] EWCA Civ 201, paragraph 26, applying *MA (Somalia) v Secretary of State for the Home Department* [2010] UKSC 49

matter on the papers[501]. Both the FTT[502] and the UT[503] are empowered to suspend the decision of the FTT pending the outcome of the appeal.

UT powers on appeal

Where the UT concludes that the FTT has erred in law, it may (but need not)[504] set the decision (or part of it) aside, and either remit the case to the FTT for re-determination, or re-make the decision itself. Where the UT remits the case to the FTT, it may direct that the case be re-heard by a fresh panel, and may give procedural directions. Where the UT re-makes the decision itself, it may make any decision which the FTT could make, and may make such findings of fact as it considers appropriate[505].

Excluded Decisions

Certain decisions are classed as excluded decisions, and are not amenable to review or appeal[506]. The relevant excluded decisions for the purposes of this book are:

- A decision to refuse to review, or to review, an earlier decision under rule 47 FTT Rules.
- A decision to take no action, or not to take any particular action, in light of a review of an earlier decision under rule 47 FTT Rules.

---

501 Rule 34 UT Rules. The UT must have regard to any view expressed by a party when deciding whether to hold a hearing to consider any matter, and the form of any such hearing.

502 Rule 5(3) (l) FTT Rules

503 Rule 5(3)(m) UT Rules

504 But is not required to do so: see for example *AA v Bristol City Council* [2025] UKUT 10 (AAC)

505 Section 12 TCEA

506 Section 11 TCEA; Appeals (Excluded Decisions) Order 2009

- A decision to set aside an earlier decision, in light of a review of an earlier decision under rule 47 FTT Rules[507].
- A decision to refer, or not to refer, a matter to the UT to be re-decided, further to an earlier decision having been reviewed and set aside under rule 47 FTT Rules.
- A decision which has been set aside further to a review under rule 47 FTT Rules (even if set aside after the commencement of an appeal).

The purpose of excluding these decisions from being amenable to appeal is to prevent an appeal being brought against a review decision, where it should be brought instead against the earlier, substantive decision[508].

The only route for a party to challenge the above excluded decisions is by way of an application for judicial review. Such an application should not be brought in the High Court, but in the UT[509], using Form JR1. An application for judicial review must be made promptly, and must be delivered to the UT so that it is received no later than 3 months after the FTT's decision[510]. The UT has the power to extend the time limit[511].

---

507 Save that where an FTT decision has been reviewed and set aside under section 9(4)(c) TCEA, the decision to set aside can be further reviewed only for the purposes of correcting accidental errors in that decision, pursuant to section 9(4)(a) TCEA.

508 *LM v London Borough of Lewisham* [2009] UKUT 204 (AAC), paragraph 14

509 Section 16 TCEA

510 Rule 28 UT Rules. An application for judicial review may be made after the 2-month time limit if it is made within 1 month of the date on which the FTT sent written reasons for a decision, or notification that an application to set aside a decision has been unsuccessful (provided that the application to set aside was made in time) (see rule 28(3) UT Rules.

511 Rule 28(7) UT Rules

MORE BOOKS BY LAW BRIEF PUBLISHING

A selection of our other titles available now:-

'A Practical Guide to Probation Breaches and Other Applications' by Mark Thomas
'A Practical Guide to Remarriage and Divorce' by Cordelia Williams & Claire Howard
'A Practical Guide to Privacy, Transparency, Reporting Restrictions and Closed Proceedings in the Court of Protection' by Laura Mannering
'Beaumont on Barristers – A Guide to Defending Disciplinary Proceedings (Second Edition)' by Marc Beaumont
'A Practical Guide to Payments for Environmental Services' by Ben Sharples
'A Practical Guide to the Law of Pregnancy and Maternity at Work' by Rebecca Thomas
'A Practical Guide to Redundancy – Second Edition' by Philip Hyland & Collette Moore
'A Practical Guide to International Issues for Scottish Family Lawyers' by Susie Mountain, Donna McKay, Ken MacDonald
'A Practical Guide to the Law on Deprivation of Liberty' by Ben Troke
'A Practical Guide to Rights over Airspace and Subsoil – Second Edition' by Daniel Gatty
'A Practical Guide to the Law in Relation to Inquests' by Ramya Nagesh
'A Practical Guide to the Construction and Rectification of Wills and Trust Instruments (Second Edition)' by Edward Hewitt
'A Practical Guide to Data Protection in Social Housing' by Clare Paterson
'A Practical Guide to Spousal Maintenance – Second Edition' by Liz Cowell
'A Practical Guide to International Parental Child Abduction Law (England and Wales)' by Dr Onyója Momoh
'A Practical Guide to Deprivation of British Citizenship' by Sean Ell
'A Practical Guide to Commercial Property Service Charges' by Rachel Garton
'A Practical Guide to Clinical Negligence – Third Edition' by Geoffrey Simpson-Scott (Geoff)
'A Practical Guide to the Rights of Grandparents in Children Proceedings – Second Edition' by Stuart Barlow

'The Electronic Communications Code: A Practical Guide – Second Edition' by Kerry Bretherton KC, James Castle, Mark Loveday
'A Practical Guide to the Independent School Standards – September 2023 Edition' by Sarah McKimm
'A Practical Guide to Estate Administration and Crypto Assets' by Richard Marshall
'A Practical Guide to Parental Alienation in Private and Public Law Children Cases' by Sam King QC & Frankie Shama
'Contested Heritage – Removing Art from Land and Historic Buildings' by Richard Harwood QC, Catherine Dobson, David Sawtell
'The Limits of Separate Legal Personality: When Those Running a Company Can Be Held Personally Liable for Losses Caused to Third Parties Outside of the Company' by Dr Mike Wilkinson
'A Practical Guide to Transgender Law' by Robin Moira White & Nicola Newbegin
'A Practical Guide to 'Stranded Spouses' in Family Law' by Mani Singh Basi
'A Practical Guide to Residential Freehold Conveyancing' by Lorraine Richardson
'A Practical Guide to Pensions on Divorce for Lawyers' by Bryan Scant
'A Practical Guide to Challenging Sham Marriage Allegations in Immigration Law' by Priya Solanki
'A Practical Guide to Digital Communications Evidence in Criminal Law' by Sam Willis
'A Practical Guide to Legal Rights in Scotland' by Sarah-Jane Macdonald
'A Practical Guide to New Build Conveyancing' by Paul Sams & Rebecca East
'A Practical Guide to Inherited Wealth on Divorce' by Hayley Trim
'A Practical Guide to Practice Direction 12J and Domestic Abuse in Private Law Children Proceedings' by Rebecca Cross & Malvika Jaganmohan
'A Practical Guide to Confiscation and Restraint' by Narita Bahra QC, John Carl Townsend, David Winch
'A Practical Guide to the Law of Forests in Scotland' by Philip Buchan
'A Practical Guide to Health and Medical Cases in Immigration Law' by Rebecca Chapman & Miranda Butler
'A Practical Guide to Bad Character Evidence for Criminal Practitioners by Aparna Rao
'A Practical Guide to Extradition Law post-Brexit' by Myles Grandison et al
'A Practical Guide to Hoarding and Mental Health for Housing Lawyers' by Rachel Coyle

'Stephens on Contractual Indemnities' by Richard Stephens

'A Practical Guide to the EU Succession Regulation' by Richard Frimston

'A Practical Guide to Solicitor and Client Costs – Second Edition' by Robin Dunne

'Constructive Dismissal – Practice Pointers and Principles' by Benjimin Burgher

'A Practical Guide to Religion and Belief Discrimination Claims in the Workplace' by Kashif Ali

'A Practical Guide to the Law of Medical Treatment Decisions' by Ben Troke

'Fundamental Dishonesty and QOCS in Personal Injury Proceedings: Law and Practice' by Jake Rowley

'A Practical Guide to the Law in Relation to School Exclusions' by Charlotte Hadfield & Alice de Coverley

'A Practical Guide to Divorce for the Silver Separators' by Karin Walker

'The Right to be Forgotten – The Law and Practical Issues' by Melissa Stock

'A Practical Guide to Planning Law and Rights of Way in National Parks, the Broads and AONBs' by James Maurici QC, James Neill et al

'A Practical Guide to Election Law' by Tom Tabori

'A Practical Guide to the Law in Relation to Surrogacy' by Andrew Powell

'A Practical Guide to Claims Arising from Fatal Accidents – Second Edition' by James Patience

'A Practical Guide to Asbestos Claims' by Jonathan Owen & Gareth McAloon

'A Practical Guide to Stamp Duty Land Tax in England and Northern Ireland' by Suzanne O'Hara

'A Practical Guide to the Law of Farming Partnerships' by Philip Whitcomb

'A Practical Guide to the Law of Unlawful Eviction and Harassment – Second Edition' by Stephanie Lovegrove

'A Practical Guide to Costs in Personal Injury Claims – Second Edition' by Matthew Hoe

'A Practical Guide to the General Data Protection Regulation (GDPR) – Second Edition' by Keith Markham

'A Practical Guide to Working with Litigants in Person and McKenzie Friends in Family Cases' by Stuart Barlow

'Protecting Unregistered Brands: A Practical Guide to the Law of Passing Off' by Lorna Brazell

'A Practical Guide to Secondary Liability and Joint Enterprise Post-Jogee' by Joanne Cecil & James Mehigan

'A Practical Guide to the Pre-Action RTA Claims Protocol for Personal Injury Lawyers' by Antonia Ford

'A Practical Guide to Neighbour Disputes and the Law' by Alexander Walsh

'A Practical Guide to Coercive Control for Legal Practitioners and Victims' by Rachel Horman

'A Practical Guide to the Law of Driverless Cars – Second Edition'

by Alex Glassbrook, Emma Northey & Scarlett Milligan

'A Practical Guide to TOLATA Claims' by Greg Williams

'A Practical Guide to Elderly Law – Second Edition' by Justin Patten

'A Practical Guide to Responding to Housing Disrepair and Unfitness Claims' by Iain Wightwick

'A Practical Guide to the Law of Bullying and Harassment in the Workplace' by Philip Hyland

'How to Be a Freelance Solicitor: A Practical Guide to the SRA-Regulated Freelance Solicitor Model' by Paul Bennett

'A Practical Guide to Prison Injury Claims' by Malcolm Johnson

'A Practical Guide to Advising Clients at the Police Station' by Colin Stephen McKeown-Beaumont

'A Practical Guide to Antisocial Behaviour Injunctions – Second Edition' by Iain Wightwick

'Practical Mediation: A Guide for Mediators, Advocates, Advisers, Lawyers, and Students in Civil, Commercial, Business, Property, Workplace, and Employment Cases' by Jonathan Dingle with John Sephton

'The Mini-Pupillage Workbook' by David Boyle

'A Practical Guide to Crofting Law' by Brian Inkster

'A Practical Guide to the Law of Domain Names and Cybersquatting' by Andrew Clemson

'A Practical Guide to the Law of Gender Pay Gap Reporting' by Harini Iyengar

'NHS Whistleblowing and the Law' by Joseph England

'Employment Law and the Gig Economy' by Nigel Mackay & Annie Powell

'A Practical Guide to Noise Induced Hearing Loss (NIHL) Claims' by Andrew Mckie, Ian Skeate, Gareth McAloon

'An Introduction to Beauty Negligence Claims – A Practical Guide for the Personal Injury Practitioner' by Greg Almond

'Intercompany Agreements for Transfer Pricing Compliance' by Paul Sutton

'Zen and the Art of Mediation' by Martin Plowman

'A Practical Guide to Adoption for Family Lawyers' by Graham Pegg

'A Practical Guide to Industrial Disease Claims' by Andrew Mckie & Ian Skeate
'A Practical Guide to Conducting a Sheriff Court Proof' by Andrew Stevenson
'A Practical Guide to Vicarious Liability' by Mariel Irvine
'A Practical Guide to Applications for Landlord's Consent and Variation of Leases' by Mark Shelton
'A Practical Guide to Relief from Sanctions Post-Mitchell and Denton' by Peter Causton
'A Practical Guide to Equity Release for Advisors' by Paul Sams
'A Practical Guide to Financial Services Claims' by Chris Hegarty
'A Practical Guide to Financial Ombudsman Service Claims' by Adam Temple & Robert Scrivenor
'A Practical Guide to Running Housing Disrepair and Cavity Wall Claims – Second Edition' by Andrew Mckie & Ian Skeate
'A Practical Guide to Holiday Sickness Claims – Second Edition' by Andrew Mckie & Ian Skeate
'Arguments and Tactics for Personal Injury and Clinical Negligence Claims' by Dorian Williams
'A Practical Guide to Drone Law' by Rufus Ballaster, Andrew Firman, Eleanor Clot
'On Experts: CPR35 for Lawyers and Experts' by David Boyle
'An Introduction to Personal Injury Law' by David Boyle

These books and more are available to order online direct from the publisher at www.lawbriefpublishing.com, where you can also read free sample chapters. For any queries, call us on 0844 587 2383 or email us at mail@lawbriefpublishing.com.

Our books are all generally in stock at www.amazon.co.uk with free next day delivery for Prime members, and at good legal bookshops such as Wildy & Sons.

We are regularly launching new books in our series of practical day-to-day practitioners' guides. Visit our website and join our free newsletter to be kept informed and to receive special offers, free chapters, etc.

You can also follow us on Twitter at www.twitter.com/lawbriefpub.

www.ingramcontent.com/pod-product-compliance
Lightning Source LLC
LaVergne TN
LVHW022048200926
848481LV00003B/827
* 9 7 8 1 9 1 6 6 9 8 7 5 8 *